be YOUtiful

A Collection of Body Image Stories for Every Body, Shape, Size, Color & Ability
Vol 1

by
Yaisa Mann
& Contributors

Copyright © 2017 by Yaisa Mann

Logo Design by
Cover and Layout Design by Moore Marketing and Communications, LLC
All rights reserved.

In accordance with the U.S. Copyright Act of 1976, scanning, uploading, or electronic sharing of any part of this book, audio, written, or e-published is strictly prohibited and unlawful. No part of this book may be reproduced in any form by any means, including photocopying, electronic, mechanical, recording, or by any information storage and retrieval systems without permission in writing by the copyright owner.

Published by
Pigeon Toed Publishing
Norman, Oklahoma

Bulk copies or group sales of this book are available by contacting yaisa@swagherfitness.com or by calling (405) 473-1566.

FIRST EDITION PRINTED JULY 2017.
Printed in USA

Mann, Yaisa
BeYouTiful: A Collection of Body Image Stories for Every Body, Shape, Size, Color and Ability. Vol. 1
First Edition.

Library of Congress Control Number: 2017944335
1. Self-Esteem 2. Image 3. Body 4. Love 5. Beauty 6. Stories 7. Positivity

Issued also as an ebook.

ISBN: 978-0-9975511-0-5

BeYouTiful
A Collection of Body Image Stories for Every Body, Shape, Size and Ability

PAGE

Introduction   9
by Yaisa Mann

Foreward   15
by Stephanie D. Moore

The Importance of the Engagement in Self-Care for   18
Multi-Cultural Women Pursuing Higher Education
by Nina Ellis-Hervey, PhD, LSSP, NCSP; Ashley Doss, MAIO-Cert; DeShae Gatti, MA/SP, School Psychology Doctoral Student; Aubrey McKenzie, BS/P, School Psychology Doctoral Student; Juliet Aura, BS/P, School Psychology Doctoral Student

Loving The Skin I'm In   38
by Yaisa Mann

BeYou   54
by Candace Liger

It Wasn't Really a Weight Problem   78
by Julie Shapiro

Behind the Mask   92
by Dee Dee Grayson

Housewife to Harvard: God Has an Extraordinary Plan   106
by Allyson Reneau

Healing and Restoration: How a Journey to Heal Myself   112
Led Me to Help Others
by Jennifer Armstrong

Getting Fit In Every Facet of Life: 122
How Getting Healthy Changed My Life
by Carlie Carpio

The Utilization of Social Media to Increase Self-Esteem   134
and Alleviate the Obesity Epidemic in Multicultural Women
by Nina Ellis-Hervey, PhD, LSSP, NCSP

More Than Able: The Power in Allowing One's Abilities   150
To Guide the Journey
by Elizabeth Reeve

About the Contributors   166

Pigeon Toed
Publishing

How beautiful upon the mountains are the feet of him who brings good news, who publishes peace, who brings good news of happiness, who publishes salvation, who says to Zion, "Your God reigns."
Isaiah 52:7

be YOU tiful

DEDICATION

To my two sons, Jalen & Josiah and my extended family.
It is also dedicated to all of the girls and women who struggle to love themselves and are afraid to be who God made them to be. And last but not least, to my daughter Jael, who I pray will love herself fiercely.

beYOUtiful

www.beyoutifulbooks.com

Book Raves & Reviews

Intriguing, interesting, inspiring, and insightful! If you have ever questioned yourself as a woman and your body image then this is the book for you.

TaKisha L. Lovelace
MINISTER AND HEALTH COACH

BeYOUtiful, an intimation that you're not alone. That you can achieve your goals and learn how to accept YOU as God created you.

Arlene Coleman
CERTIFIED PERSONAL TRAINER AND BARRE INSTRUCTOR

The book opens with a slightly academic but engaging blitz through the whys and hows of caring for the mental, physical and spiritual self. The style then changes and the authors take the reader through a series of personal stories on their struggles with various image issues. The chapters are emotional but the authors manage to masterfully temper challenges with successes. The result is a well-balanced read; not too overwhelming, not too idealistic. Additionally, the linguistic styles employed are vast, further enhancing the rollercoaster feeling one gets through the chapters. Beyoutiful is a delightful little book that a wide range of academic and non-academic readers will find enlightening and thoroughly uplifting.

Dr George Mwenda, PhD
MICROBIOLOGIST

Body Image is a hot topic but it is muddled with different meanings.

Introduction
by Yaisa Mann

The question,
"What does it mean for women to engage in the pursuit of being and feeling beautiful?"

This is the heart and core of this edited interdisciplinary anthology of non-fiction essays by women on the topic of body image with a focus on self care, social media, fitness, skin color, motherhood, selfhood and identity.

beYOUtiful

Body image is a hot topic but is muddled with different meanings. Most relate body image to eating disorders, weight, and external appearance but it's much more than that. It is the perception that one has about his or herself; it can be either positive or negative. Typically included in beauty are characteristics like weight, shape, size, hair texture, skin color, facial features, and etc. In order to examine beauty this book embodies stories with a focus on "BeYOUtiful," which means you're beautiful when you choose to be yourself.

I have been a body image researcher, writer, and lecturer for over twenty years; several works have broken ground in critical embodiment studies approaches, including Ayana Byrd and Akiba Solomon's Naked: Black Women Bare All Their Skin, Hair, Lips, and Other Parts (2005), Ophira Edut's Body Outlaws: Rewriting the Rules of Beauty and Body Image (2003), and Debra Gimlin's Body Work: Beauty and Self Image in American Culture (2002). However, no single book has heretofore gathered the voices and experiences of women to discuss body image and the practice of being you.
The field of body image is a relatively new field of study and was first coined by Austrian neurologist and psychoanalyst Paul Schilder in his book The Image and Appearance of the Human Body in 1939. Body image is defined as one's perception of their appearance based on how one feels about themselves and also how they feel others see them. This view is shaped by external factors like family, peers, culture and the media.

My life changed once I heard the term body image while working as a teaching assistant for Introduction to Women's Studies at the University of Oklahoma. I had gotten my Bachelors and Master Degrees in English and African American Studies from California State University, Fresno. I figured that I'd become an English professor and writer, but I was just following the path of what I thought that I was supposed to do. I set out to master the English language.

www.beyoutifulbooks.com

> GROWING UP I WAS TEASED ABOUT THE WAY I TALKED. I TALKED TOO FAST AND LOUD WITH EXPRESSIVE MOVEMENT OF NECK ROLLING AND MY HANDS WAVING IN THE AIR. MY FEELINGS GOT HURT EVERY TIME I GOT TEASED, SO I BECAME QUIET AND SMILED ALL OF THE TIME.

I knew that I had a voice and things to say but somehow understood that I was going to be all right.

Years later once I set foot in the Women's Studies class, I got my voice. I knew that I would teach this subject, learn more, and talk about all of the issues from relationships, domestic violence, wage gap, work family balance and body image. The atmosphere in this class was a lot different than in most other college classes. The majority of students were female, lively and ready to engage in discussions. The readings: "The Opt Out Revolution" by Lisa Belkin, "White Privilege: Unpacking My Invisible Knapsack," by Peggy McIntosh, "Alpha Girls: Understanding the New American Girl and How She is Changing the World," and "Reviving Ophelia: Saving the Selves of Adolescent Girls," by Mary Pipher really stood out to me. These readings gave an account of the status of girls and women with statistics and commentary but they also made students realize that the women they were reading about were their grandmothers and mother's generation and could be them.

What stood out most was that women learn that they must follow certain guidelines and standards of behavior and beauty according to their race and class or they fail at being a woman. The ideal woman, as portrayed by the media and popular culture is thin, white and quiet. Some other features may include large breasts and blonde hair. This image is presented to girls through toys such as baby dolls who mature into skinny Barbie dolls. As a result, this image steals young girls' innocence, and affects most women on a daily basis.

During the end of the semester when students presented their projects on women's issues varying from healthcare, education, and politics though all presentations were informative and eye opening the body image one caught my attention and really helped me to align up my body image perspective. The group showed a short video sponsored by the Dove True Beauty Campaign called Evolution. The video starts off with a white woman on the set of a photo shoot getting her hair and makeup done. She is above average in looks, not a high fashion model that is stick thin but a print model for catalogs and commercials. After she is made-up there is a photo shoot and then the evolution begins. The image is transferred to a computer and then the digital design crew begins doing Photoshop on the model. Her neck is stretched and collar bone and veins smoothed out. Her hair is thickened to show no gaps or fly-aways. Her face is thinned out. Her checks are sunken in and jawbone made more defined. Her lips are plumped up and made to be pouty and pursed. Her eyes are widened and eyelashes thickened and elongated. Any wrinkles or blemishes are erased. I'm witnessing Photoshop for the first time and I can't believe what I'm seeing. That presentation was an eye opener to understanding body image in a profound way and fueled my passion to help others.

I was invited to be a visiting lecturer for the Women's and Gender Studies Program at the University of Oklahoma based on my substantial research and work in popular culture, beauty culture and body image. I developed program curriculum for the first body image course ever taught at the University of Oklahoma to meet university and departmental needs, and designed it to fulfill the general education requirement: Body Image Versus Reality: Popular Culture and the Beauty Myth (2008). This class was highlighted in the OU Daily as one of the best classes to enrich the education experience of students.

I have also developed and taught several themed oriented intersession courses: Racialicous: Race, Class, Gender and Sexuality in Girl's Studies (2010); Women, Rap, and Hip Hop Feminism (2011), Barbie Bender: Nicki Minaj Complicating Race, Gender, Sexuality and Pink Femininity (2012); Freshman 15: Attaining and Maintaining a Healthy Body Image (2011-2012); Beyonce Schoolin' Life: Politicizing the

Pop Cultural Diva (2012); Bands A Make Her Dance: Shaking the Meaning Out of Miley Cyrus' Twerking (2012).

I am very active in the popular culture community and am a guest blogger for About Face Media Literacy which is a nonprofit organization that equips girls and women with literacy skills to resist media messages that affect their self esteem and body image. I was invited as one the most influential's professors and the University of Oklahoma to give a lecture for Great Night of the Orators (2014). I was featured in the eleventh edition of Our Bodies Ourselves (2011) and have worked with Reality TV celebrities Jonathan Kayne from Project Runway, Ginger Wells from America's Next Top Model, and Allie Ishcomer and Lisa Mosely from Biggest Loser.

The media and advertising play a huge role in influencing what both men and women view as beauty. The vision of this book will serve as social activism and conscious raising where readers will learn to counter the beast of low self-esteem, objectification, an unhealthy body image, eating disorders, fear, shame, and realize the beauty of being who God created you to be.

Did you know that the average American woman is 5'4' tall and weighs 145 pounds? And the average American model is 5'11' and weighs 117 pounds. The average model is then 7" taller, but 23 pounds lighter than the average woman. Surprisingly models make up only 2% of the entire female population, but they create the beauty standard for 98% of women struggling with their bodies.

The struggle is so real that women resort to dieting and negative self-talk, which ultimately leads to anxiety, depression, low self-esteem, an unhealthy body image, disordered eating, and undiagnosed mental illness.

be YOUtiful

> Many women suffer in silence every day thinking, "If I only was like _____ (who ever is the beauty standard), then I'd be good. Does your story sound familiar?

www.beyoutifulbooks.com

Foreward
WHAT THEY SAW & WHAT I BELIEVED
by Stephanie D. Moore

"I'm glad I'm not dark-skinned."
My little sister, one day after swimming.
I wished and wished I had lighter skin.

"I'm going to knock the black off you."
I was on the tetherball court.
Her words embarrassed me and I thought, "Why am I so Black?"

"Ooh, you are starting to get love handles."
I was 16, working at McDonald's. I didn't know what those were but when
I found out, I believed I was extremely fat.

"Those glasses look like Coke Bottles!"
We were having dinner and a family member joked about my glasses.
I was ashamed and thought my glasses made me ugly.

"Don't nobody want a fat girl!"
A boy I admired in middle school joked about me to his friends.
I cried myself home and ate all I could to comfort my darkened mind.

be YOUtiful

Echoes of the ugly words people spoke to me about my body image often found themselves improperly placed on shelves of low self-esteem that somehow managed to always have real estate in my mind and heart. It started when I was a little girl but as I aged, so did my low self-esteem. These echoes often reverbed and grew manifesting themselves into poor decisions, exaggerated reactions and erroneous assumptions.

So many times, I tried to erase them, or replace them with positive affirmations. Which worked for a while, but seemed ineffective without the help of Jesus on my side. There wasn't one person walking this earth that could make me see life in a positive way, assuring me that they would never leave… but Jesus.

> IT WASN'T UNTIL I MET THE LORD IN AN INTIMATE WAY (THROUGH STUDY, PRAYER AND WORSHIP) DID I BEGIN TO TRULY SEE MYSELF DIFFERENTLY AND TRANSFORM MY MIND. THAT TRANSFORMATION LED TO CHOICES THAT WERE DIRECTED BY WISDOM.

Of course, the residue of disrespect, poor body image and early abandonment by my father still have effect. The only difference is now they encourage me to uplift others and help them meet their destiny.

When I found Christ, I discovered my life. The first book I wrote was 'Echoes: Tired, Worn Out and Over It… Ignoring the Echoes and Listening to God's Voice.' Beyond the echoes of low self-esteem were the echoes of molestation, rape, gang violence, death and drug abuse. After a failed marriage and totaling six cars in one year, I couldn't imagine being "good" to or for anyone. I spiraled down a tunnel of drug use and poor decision.

Today, I have written eight books, including a coloring book for little girls I co-authored with my daughter, Dallas. I have created several community focused programs for women and teens that are are

www.beyoutifulbooks.com

becoming national brands… they are important to me and I don't mind giving all that I am to share this wisdom the Lord has given me, with them. Finally, I own a successful marketing company serving all manner of clients, from spa owners to politicians all over the nation.

I am not perfect, but I have learned to passionately love my imperfections. They are a critical element in the unique recipe God designed when creating me. They keep me honorable to God, humble, honest and hard-working. They keep me hungry to do more and to help others become more.

The version of me God made is enough!
I am unique and beautiful, perfectly imperfect in every way.
This is what I believe and this is what I see.
I BELIEVE!

"For my grace is sufficient, for in your weakness is my strength made perfect."
2 Corinthians 12:9

Nina Ellis-Hervey

Ph.D., L.P., N.C.S.P., L.S.S.P., C.P.C.
Licensed Psychologist #37316
Licensed Specialist in School Psychology #70264
Certified Professional Life Coach
Associate Professor
School Psychology Assessment Center Director
School Psychology Program
Human Services
Stephen F. Austin State University

THE IMPORTANCE OF THE ENGAGEMENT IN SELF-CARE FOR MULTI-CULTURAL WOMEN PURSUING HIGHER EDUCATION

by Nina Ellis-Hervey, Ph.D., L.P., N.C.S.P., L.S.S.P., C.P.C.;
Ashley Doss, MAIO-Cert;
DeShae Gatti, MA/SP, School Psychology Doctoral Student;
Aubrey McKenzie, BS/P, School Psychology Doctoral Student;
Juliet Aura, BS/P, School Psychology Doctoral Student

Although women are making great gains in higher education, and even surpassing men in some areas, women are still the minority in a male-dominated world. Disparity is still ever present as it pertains to gender and race. This disparity is seen in homes, jobs, and the classroom. Sadly, women who need self-care the most, struggle with allowing themselves the opportunity more than their male counterparts (Baker, 2011). Women of color have the highest reported levels of stress in the U.S. (Perry, Harp, & Oser, 2013). This stress only increases in the world of higher education (Maton, Wimms, Grant, Wittig, Rogers, & Vasquez, 2011). Multi-cultural women face many internal battles, struggling to be recognized as not only equal to their male counterparts but also to their female counterparts. These stressors may often lead into an abyss of long days and sleepless nights.

> WOMEN MAY RESORT TO WEARING CONCEALER TO HIDE THE EVER-PRESENT DARK CIRCLES AROUND THEIR EYES, FORCING A SMILE, ONLY TO CLOSE THE DAY WITH MENTAL BREAKDOWNS OR EVEN CRYING.

There is a battle to be heard in a world that still does not value the voice of women the way it should, particularly women of color. Though the pursuit of higher education can be quite difficult alone, women of color face many adversities that add to that stress. However this population is least likely to seek out psychological services while progressing in their education (Hyun, Quinn, Madon, & Lustig, 2006).

Since the 1960s, an increasing amount of women have enrolled in degree-granting institutions in the pursuit of a higher education (Chien, 2014). A greater percentage of women have enrolled in higher education institutions and a nearly equal balance of males and females are graduating from these institutions. Women often face greater barriers in their pursuit of higher education as expectations of them to stay home and raise their families are still prevalent in a majority of cultures (ICEF Monitor, 2014). This discriminating expectation for females has declined in recent years, yet it is still expected that females combine family life and studies, and are able to do all. This expectation has not halted most women's aspirations in obtaining higher education degrees, as over 1.7 million females were enrolled in post baccalaureate institutions in 2012 (National Center for Education Sciences [NCES], 2015). A contributing factor to an increase in female enrollment for higher education includes universal aspirations for schooling beyond secondary school years, the feminization of the teaching profession, greater verbal abilities of females, and effectively creating a balance between studies and home life (Klemencic & Fried, n.d.; ICEF Monitor, 2014). A struggle in creating a balance between academic studies and home life still remains. Although there has been an increased enrollment of females within higher education institutions (an increase of 42%), graduation rates between males and females are roughly equal to each other (Chien, 2014). This indicates that although female enrollment has surpassed male enrollment, graduation rates for males and females remain the same. In examining post baccalaureate enrollment rates, specifically master's degrees, 56% of women pursue this level of degree. In the pursuance of doctoral degrees, males comprise about 56% of PhD graduates and over 71% of males are employed in a research position post-graduation (Chien, 2014). This is of value as it indicates that females stop at the master's level of post baccalaureate education and the research field is predominantly male. A predominantly male research field may limit the understanding of female roles, as males may hold less interest on how females balance academic studies and home life. Including the lack of recognition by men concerning the multicultural aspect of female self-care while in pursuit of higher education.

Within the female percentage of those enrolled in higher education institutions, enrollment for women of a multicultural background has also climbed. From 1975 to 2012, enrollment rates for Hispanic women has increased from 12% to 41.7% and for Black women it has risen from 15.9% to 38.7% (for comparison, White women percentages have risen from 22.5% to 46%; NCES, 2015). Although the rates of multicultural women enrolling in higher education institutions has risen, few research studies fully explore development (particularly leadership development) of multicultural women in academia (Davis & Maldonado, 2015). In examining leadership roles and development for multicultural women, a primary limitation is the focus on traditional leadership roles adopted by White males in a corporate environment. Specifically, research on African American women is even more limited, being subsumed into feminist literature as a sliver of the feminist movement (Davis & Maldonado, 2015). White females tend to be at the forefront of concern when examining graduation and enrollment rates in academia, leaving women of a multicultural background out of the spotlight with the "hope" to be acknowledged. This has led to African American women finding themselves more divided in the majority culture, as their needs and successes are often overlooked in the face of White women's accomplishments. It is important that White women recognize the subculture of African American and multicultural women overall and lift up their accomplishments beyond the majority feminist movement.

Stress, depression, and other mental illnesses are a common problem among women in the United States. Females are twice as likely to be diagnosed with depression and anxiety as males (American Psychological Association [APA], 2016; Center for Disease Control [CDC], 2013). Some reports convey that although two times as many are diagnosed, between 30% and 50% of women diagnosed with depression are misdiagnosed, leading to a misuse in prescription medications (APA, 2016). Other reports show many women are underdiagnosed, where only two in five individuals experiencing a mood disorder seek treatment within the first year of onset (World Health Organization [WHO], 2016). Stress is a common experience for all individuals, especially in a more fast-paced society. Individuals under stress may experience it in different ways, including not eating or eating too much, feelings of no control, forgetfulness, headaches, lack of energy, lack of focus, difficulty completing tasks, low self-esteem, short tempers, changes in sleep patterns, upset stomach, and general aches and pains (Office on Women's Health [OWH], 2012). Overall, it is believed roughly 12% of the population of women experience mental health illnesses including depression, anxiety, and stress (CDC, 2013). In the goal of pursuing higher education, these rates climbs as reports indicate 12% to 18% of the college student population are treated for mental health disorders (Flatt, 2013). However, this number is believed to be higher, as over 75% of college students have self-reported that they do not seek treatment when experiencing these symptoms.

The Center for Disease Control (2013) has reported lower depression and anxiety percentages for individuals of a multicultural background (at rates including 4.57% for African Americans and 5.17% for Hispanics, with a slightly higher percentage of 6.51% for Whites). However, recent research has begun to reflect that these reports may be inaccurate as understanding the multicultural factors in treating for depression, anxiety, and stress may not be considered when seeking treatment (Jack, Ali, & Dias, 2013). A primary issue with this inaccurate reporting is misdiagnoses. Statistically, multicultural women are at a greater risk for mental health illnesses because of lower socioeconomic status, racial and ethnic discriminations, lower education, segregation into low status high-stress jobs, larger families, poorer health, and single parenthood compared to White women (APA, 2016). It is interesting to note that many researchers recognize the greater risk to African American women, Hispanic women, and Native American women, yet the overall statistics reflect higher depressive rates among White men and women than those with a multicultural background. The inconsistencies discovered in research reflects inaccurate reporting on statistics, so it is recommended that individuals focus on increasing awareness and understanding of intersectionality, self-reflexivity, and accountability (Jack et al., 2013). Intersectionality occurs when multiple sources of oppression are combined to disempower groups of women in a complex and interacting manner (Jack et al., 2013, p. 3). It is difficult to identify and draw to the surface for many women but is oppressive and overbearing in nature. Self-reflexivity is identified as the stance of the researchers' own social identities which shape what the researcher identifies as worthy of study and what is seen more readily versus what goes unnoticed (Jack et al., 2013). Accountability is a greater need for feminist work to strive for social transformation and equality across groups-including at a multicultural level (Jack et al., 2013). Each of these three factors identify the multicultural aspect of feminism and recognizing the stress women encounter in the workforce and education field. As a whole, multicultural differences may often be unaccounted for and passed off as unimportant or unnecessary when considering "the bigger picture." In truth, multiculturalism is part of the bigger picture and it is important to understand the trials and tribulations that women of ethnic backgrounds other than White women face on a regular basis. The oppression and silence women of ethnic background endure needs to be pulled from the shadows so that treatments may be identified in counteracting stress, anxiety, depression, and other mental health disorders.

It is suggested that college students with less understanding of stress management should practice better self-care habits (Fogle & Pettijohn, 2012). Underrepresented minorities, people of color, lower socioeconomic status, those who are first-generational students, and single-parents are the most at risk for stress (Bulgar & Watson, 2006). Research studies have also shown that women of color are more likely to die from cancers and other illnesses than their counterparts. Job discrimination, gender wage gaps, and inadequate health care all contribute to increasing these health risks.

Women are engrained to take on roles as the housekeeper, the nurturer, and are usually the one most likely to volunteer when another is in need (Mayor, 2015). These extensive roles often reduce the amount of time focused on personal care (Mayor, 2015).

Fogle and Pettijohn (2012) suggested that male college students have less stress than females. Furthermore, traditional students practice greater self-care than non-traditional students (Hermon & Davis, 2004). The traditional student is often described as a young middle to upper class White male or female, does not have children, are married with children, or have support of immediate family and friends. The traditional student may engage in greater physical care such as taking part in regular exercise (i.e., running) and are more likely to seek medical attention from family physicians or on-campus medical personnel (Hermon & Davis, 2004). Traditional students have a greater likelihood to de-stress, with vacations, or outings with friends and family. However the non-traditional students, such as single parents, Latinos, or African Americans, are less likely to partake in physical exercise and have a decreased likelihood to see physicians (Lott, 2008). This lack of self-care stems from the lack of access (Lott, 2008; Lott & Saxton, 2002). Women of color are more likely to come from lower middle class to poverty-stricken families, and do not have access to the same treatments as their more privileged counterparts. For healthcare, the average woman of color has government insurance, such as Medicaid or no insurance at all, limiting her from seeking medical help (Lott, 2008).

> Moreover, one in five women of color will wait over 60 days to see a physician after a positive mammogram as opposed to White women who will see a physician within 30 days. Roughly 83% of White women receive treatment for these illnesses compared to only 69% of women of color (United States Department of Health and Human Services, 2013).

Proper self-care is a myriad of things, with knowledge of the advantages to self-care at the core. As aforementioned, this knowledge also comes from access, and lower socioeconomic persons (predominately persons of color) have lesser access to books, quality foods, adequate schools, or equal healthcare (Lott, 2008; Lott, & Saxton 2002). These barriers do not mean those in a lower socioeconomic group cannot gain the understanding of self-care and its importance, it does however make the feat more tedious than their White counterparts (Chuy & Redfield, 2014). The primary piece of understanding self-care is the knowledge that stress can be emotionally, mentally, and physically exhausting. The woman of color has an immediate societal stress from the time of birth, the stress that they are not good enough, that there is something wrong with their hair, the depth of their voice, and the width of their nose. It is imperative for women of color to understand self-care, not just to store it in their memory, and sink into societal complacency, but to use it as a catalyst to spread the knowledge and correct the misconceptions. Although each woman learns the knowledge differently, either through familial support and stability since the time of birth, or they have discovered it through their own personal journey in life, the key is to spread the knowledge and support each other in proper self-care. Every women is worthy of relaxation, good health care, and emotional, physical, and mental stability, regardless of societal standards.

One of the strategies that have been used by multicultural women is empowerment (Doubova, Infante-Castaneda, Martinez-Vega, & Perez-Cuevas, 2012). Empowerment involves having resources available for self-care. Health-oriented empowerment is a continuous process, based on background information such as knowledge, health education, initiative, and access to services. Physician-patient communication is key. Empowerment promotes self-care autonomy, which increases durability of behavioral changes related to health (e. g., the use of birth control methods and attendance of prenatal care; Doubova et al., 2012).

Cultural trends may have been enhanced and/or transformed by the increased prominence of complementary and alternative medicine (CAM); which often includes a focus on self-determination and self-responsibility for achieving health and wellbeing (Broom, Meurk, Adams, & Sibbritt, 2012). Broom et al. (2012) conducted a study to examine women's contemporary self-care practices and the logics underpinning their approaches to health, illness, and healing. Results concluded that although women were often positive about the prospects of being autonomous decision makers, their search for alternatives and practices of self-care can be problematic in certain cases and may be viewed as reproducing neoliberal forms of governance and their trite inequalities (Broom et al., 2012).

Essentially, although women valued their independent decision making choices and abilities, men considered it trivial and ridiculous, often ignoring this need.

Some of the strategies that women have been known to use are summarized by the Loyola University Counselling Centre and are known as the 3Rs of self-care and relaxation. The first is to Recognize your signs of stress. For example, heavy breathing, digestive changes, skin problems, and other physical ailments may be signs of stress. The second strategy is to have a Routine, including balanced meals, exercise, adequate rest, and time to spend with loved ones. Finally, Relaxation techniques include breathing exercises, meditation, and yoga. Researchers focused on the effect of religion on health and social relationships and how it improved poor health behaviors and mental health (Strawbridge, Shem, Cohen, & Kaplan, 2001). Strawbridge et al. (2001) discovered that religiosity was consistent with known gender differences in association between religious attendance and survival. A strong correlation was identified between church attendance, access to health facilities, and self-care among Appalachian women (Slusher, Withrow-Fletcher, & Hause-Whitaker, 2010). In order to feel healthy, participants needed to experience balance between the physical, mental, and spiritual realms of their lives. This balance was essential for women to survive the daily stresses of work, family, and community (Slusher et al., 2010). Strategies women employed to achieve and maintain a healthy balance included connecting with nature, integrating natural practices, and listening to spiritual guidance (Canales, 2004). These strategies are consistent with the 3R's of the Loyola University Counseling Centre. African American women going to school and pursuing higher education possess a unique challenge when it comes to self-care in that it can be extremely difficult to manage and prioritize time spent between school, work, family, and themselves (Beyer, 2013). The best way for women to exercise self-care is to have proper time management skills, allowing them to maximize their available time (Beyer, 2013). This also involves prioritizing tasks and focusing on what is most important first. An integral part of prioritizing is knowing what comes first and recognizing that each person has a different set of priorities (Bransdrud, 1997). For example, some people have also been known to opt for online classes as these save on time and allow for greater flexibility. Finally, having a strong support system works to provide access to others who are able to help out with juggling various responsibilities. For example, a family member or close friend from church who is able to babysit young children for a single woman while she attends an evening class (Beyer, 2013). These techniques can be combined with the 3 Rs above to ensure effectiveness.

Women of color have the highest reported levels of stress in the U.S. (Perry et al., 2013). A significant portion of their lives are spent shouldering the burdens of others with little concern for their own health and happiness. Furthermore, navigating a racist, sexist, and classist world is harmful for women of color. Lessening the impact of oppression is an impossible task, but centering the needs and desires of women of color allow them to exact some semblance of pleasure in their lives. Audre Lorde, a Black Feminist, theorist, and activist, famously pronounced "Caring for [oneself] is not self-indulgence, it is self-preservation…". It is imperative for women of color to understand self-care. Self-care means taking the time and action to care for your emotional, physical, or spiritual well-being. Some ways in which women of color can engage in self-care include empowerment and having the resources and knowledge of how to engage in self-care. This knowledge includes recognizing signs of stress, incorporating healthy daily routines, and utilizing relaxation techniques.

Specific steps women of color may take to engage in self-care might be joining a community and/or activity that allow them to engage with other women of color. For example, Eugene (1995) asserts that other Black women validate the experiences, perspectives, and feelings of Black women that mainstream society attempts to invalidate. By joining a community that allows women of color to engage with women like themselves, the community has the potential to serve not only as a springboard for common interests, but a support network of similar others who place importance on the well-being and development of one another. A support network provides women of color the chance to empower others through support and assistance. Although a woman may join a network in search of all-natural hair products, she may find emotional support in her newfound group as she struggles through personal trials and tribulations. Networks may initially begin with a focus of assisting others in a specific area and eventually expound into something greater. A woman may start out with finding a great hairdresser who eventually provides her with social and emotional support as she combats sexism and racism in her place of employment.

Relaxation is another, but often overlooked, method to engage in self-care ("Self-care and Relaxation," n. d.). Relaxation is an essential underpinning of a healthy lifestyle. Most of us need help to slow the quickened pace of our lives, having lost or forgotten the gentle art of calming and centering. Relaxation techniques can help in coping with everyday stress and stress related to various health problems, physically and emotionally. Relaxation techniques such as deep breathing, exercising, meditation, and yoga, are often free or low in cost, pose little risk, and can be done just about anywhere. Relaxation techniques are skills, and like other skills, they need practice. People who use these techniques frequently, are more likely to benefit from them over time.

Multicultural women must, at all times, uplift not only themselves but one another, while remembering to engage in self-care. A balance of healthy living and productive work must be established, which includes knowing when to relax and understanding the importance of taking quality time for oneself. More specifically, the importance of loving the self through a system that does not often cater to the needs of multicultural women cannot be measured by words but by reassurance and teaching of daily self-care techniques that increase motivation, self-esteem, and locus of control.

REFERENCES

American Psychological Association. (2016). Women and depression. Retrieved from http://www.apa.org/about/gr/issues/women/depression.aspx

Baker, E. K. (2003). Caring for ourselves: A therapist's guide to personal and professional well- being. Washington, D.C.: American Psychological Association.

Broom, A., Meurk, C., Adams, J., & Sibbritt, D. (2012). My health, my responsibility: Complementary medicine and self (health) care. Journal of sociology, 0, 1-16. doi: 10.1177/1440783312467098

Bransdrud, D. (1997). Tips on being a mom and nursing student. National Nurses Students Association. Retrieved from http://www.nsna.org/CareerCenter/Tipson.aspx

Bulger, S., & Watson, D. (2006). Broadening the definition of at-risk students. The Community College Enterprise, 12(2), 23-32.

Canales, M. (2004). Taking care of self: Healthcare decision making of American Indian women. Healthcare for Women International, 25, 411-435.

Center for Disease Control. (2013). Burden of mental illness. Retrieved from http://www.cdc.gov/mentalhealth/basics/burden.htm

Chien, C. L. (2014). Women in higher education. Retrieved from http://www.uis.unesco.org/education/pages/women-higher-education.aspx

Chua, A., & Redfield, J. (2014). What drives success. The New York Times retrieved from: http://www.nytimes.com/2014/01/26/opinion/sunday/what-drives-success.html?_r=0

Davis, D. R., & Maldonado, C. (2015). Shattering the glass ceiling: The leadership development of African American women in higher education. Advancing Women in Leadership, 35, 48-64. Retrieved from http://awljournal.org/vol35_2015/Davis_shattering_the_glass_ceiling.pdf

Doubova, S. V., Infante-Castaneda, C., Martinez-Vega, I, & Perez-Cuevas, R. (2012). Toward healthy aging through empowering self-care during the climacteric stage. Climacteric, 15(6), 563-572. doi: 10.3109/13697137.2011.635824

Eugene, T. M. (1995). There is a balm in Gilead: Black women and the Black church as agents of therapeutic community. Women and Therapy, 16, 55-71.
Flatt, A. K. (2013). A suffering generation: Six factors contributing to the mental

health crisis in North American higher education. College Quarterly, 16(1). Retrieved from http://www.senecacollege.ca/quarterly/2013-vol16-num01-01/flatt.html

Fogle, G. E., & Pettijohn, T. F. (2013). Stress and health habits in college students. Open Journal of Medical Psychology, 2, 61-68. doi: 10.4236/ojmp.2013.22010

Geronimus, A. T., Hicken, M. T., Pearson, J. A., Seashols, S. J., Brown, K. L., & Cruz, T. D. (2010). Do US Black Women Experience Stress-Related Accelerated Biological Aging?: A Novel Theory and First Population-Based Test of Black-White Differences in Telomere Length. Human Nature (Hawthorne, N.Y.), 21(1), 19–38. http://doi.org/10.1007/s12110-010-9078-0

Hermon, D. A., & Davis, G. A. (2004). College Student Wellness: A Comparison Between Traditional- and Nontraditional-Age Students. Journal Of College Counseling, 7(1), 32-39.

Hyun, J. K., Quinn, B. C., Madon, T., & Lustig, S. (2006). Graduate student mental health: Needs assessment and utilization of counseling services. Journal of College Student Development, 47 247-266

ICEF Monitor. (2014). Women increasingly outpacing men's higher education participation in many world markets. Retrieved from http://monitor.icef.com/2014/10/women-increasingly-outpacing-mens-higher-education-participation-many-world-markets/

Jack, D. C., Ali, A., & Dias, S. (2013). Depression in multicultural populations. In F. T. L. Leong (Series Ed.), APA Handbook of Multicultural Psychology: Volume 2 Applications and Training (pp. 1-21).

Jun, A., & Tierney, W. G. At-Risk Students and College Success: A Framework for Effective College Preparation Programs in Urban Environments.

Klemencic, M., & Fried, J. (n. d.). Demographic challenges and the future of higher education. International Higher Education, 12-14.

Lott, B. (2012). The Social Psychology of Class and Classism. American Psychologist, 67(8), 650-658. doi:10.1037/a0029369

Lott, B., & Saxon, S. (2002). The influence of ethnicity, social class, and context on judgments about U.S. women. The Journal of Social Psychology, 142(4),481-499. doi:10.1080/00224540209603913

Maton, K. I., Wimms, H. E., Grant, S. K., Wittig, M. A., Rogers, M. R., & Vasquez, M. J. T. (2011). Experiences and perspectives of African American, Latina/o, Asian American, and European American psychology graduate students: A national study. Cultural Diversity & Ethnic Minority Psychology, 17, 68–78. doi:10.1037/a002166

Mayor, E. (2015). Gender roles and traits in stress and health. Frontiers in Psychology, 6, 779. http://doi.org/10.3389/fpsyg.2015.00779

National Coalition on Black Civic Participation Black Women's Roundtable (2014) BLACK WOMEN IN THE UNITED STATES, 2014 Progress and Challenges 50 Years After the War on Poverty 50 Years After the 1964 Civil Rights Act 60 Years After Brown v. Board of Education. Retrieved from: https://www.washingtonpost.com/r/2010-2019/WashingtonPost/2014/03/27/NationalPolitics/Stories/2FinalBlackWomenintheUS20 14.pdf

Office on Women's Health. (2012). Stress and your health fact sheet. Retrieved from http://womenshealth.gov/publications/our-publications/fact-sheet/stress-your-health.html

Perry, B. L., Harp, K. L. H., & Oser, C. B. (2013). Racial and gender discrimination in the Stress Process: Implications for African American women's health and well-being. Sociological Perspectives : SP : Official Publication of the Pacific Sociological Association, 56(1), 25–48.

Self-care and Relaxation. (n. d.). In Loyola University Maryland Counseling Centre website. Retrieved from http://www.loyola.edu/department/counselingcenter/students/relaxation/relaxation

Slusher I., Withrow-Fletcher C., & Hause-Whitaker M., (2010), Appalachian women: Health belief, self-care and basic conditioning factors. Journal of cultural diversity, (17)3, 84-90.

Strawbridge W., Shema S., Cohen D. & Kaplan G. (2001), Religious attendance increases survival by improving and maintaining good health behavior, mental health and social relationships, Analysis of behavior medicine, (23)1, 68-74. doi 10.1207/515324796ABM2301-10.

U. S. Department of Education, Institute of Education Sciences, National Center for Education Statistics. (2015). Percentage of 18- to 24-year-olds enrolled in degree-granting institutions, by level of institution and sex and race/ethnicity of student: 1967 through 2012 (Table No. 302.60). Retrieved from NCES website: http://nces.ed.gov/programs/digest/d13/tables/dt13_302.60.asp

U. S. Department of Education, Institute of Education Sciences, National Center for Education Statistics. (2015). Postbaccalaureate enrollment. Retrieved from http://nces.ed.gov/programs/coe/indicator_chb.asp

World Health Organization. (2016). Gender and women's mental health. Retrieved from http://www.who.int/mental_health/prevention/genderwomen/en/

Biography of Nina Ellis

Dr. Nina Ellis-Hervey a.k.a. BeautifulBrwnBabyDol is a tenured and Associate Professor in the School Psychology Doctoral Program at Stephen F. Austin State University. She is a Licensed Psychologist, Nationally Certified School Psychologist, a Licensed Specialist in School Psychology in the state of Texas and a Certified Professional Life Coach. She is also the director of the School Psychology Assessment Center on campus. She is soon to be a Certified Personal Trainer in 2017. Her YouTube channels and website entitled "BeautifulBrwnBabyDol" and "BeautifulBrwnBabyDolTV" chronicle her more than 100lb. weight loss she has maintained for over 10 years, educational triumphs, healthy psychological tips and beauty tutorials. With over half a million subscribers (between channels), millions of video views nationally and internationally, and nearly 1 million following across networks, Dr. Nina is making her mark on the world. Her YouTube channel has recently been named as a top 10 natural hair vlog by Buzzfeed. She has also been featured in PEOPLE, Essence and Ebony magazines and the TV shows HLN News Live, the Jeff Probst Show, Inside Edition, Extra, The Grio, Refinery 29 and more! She was named a St. Louis Woman Power Player by Delux Magazine as well! Dr. Nina has even given a TED talk at the Illinois Institute of Technology. She has also spoken at many universities including Howard University, Colgate University, Albany State University, Texas State University, Illinois State University and more. Her academic works have been and are being published in the journals Learning, Media and Technology, Journal of Human Services, Educational Review, The McNair Scholarly Review, Psychology Discourse, Journal of Black Studies, Journal of Multicultural Affairs and Girls Like Us: Risk, Resilience and Healthy Development of Diverse Girls. She believes in supporting others in reaching their goals and seeing their lives as valuable in spite of any adversity they may face. She lives her life as the ultimate example of that.

Biography of Ashley Doss

Ashley Doss is a doctoral student enrolled in the School Psychology program at Stephen F. Austin State University. Before joining the program at SFASU, Ashley worked in a corporate environment, gaining experience in the concept of creating Lean processes in an organization focused on reducing wasteful procedures and understanding basic principles of Industrial/Organizational Psychology. Ashley received her Master's Certification in Industrial/Organizational Psychology before enrolling into the School Psychology program at SFASU. Changing into the field of School Psychology has provided Ashley with the opportunity to work on multiple projects, including combating obesity using social media as a platform, increasing understanding and awareness of multiculturalism, particularly understanding self-esteem in African American women, and identifying variables of the military lifestyle that impact military children. Ashley's main focus in her program of study includes counseling, assessments, consultation, behavior analysis, systems-level services, and increasing her understanding of diversity and multiculturalism. In the future, one of Ashley's plans includes focusing on being able to work with military families on a more in-depth level, creating and developing interventions and providing services that assist military families from all backgrounds to increase engagement and cohesion within the military family, fostering academic and psychological success for military children. Ashley also plans to work with multicultural families, increasing awareness and engagement and fostering greater academic success with underserved and overserved communities within the school system. Other plans include focusing on systems-level interventions and services to provide parent training, tier 1 services, and increased support between schools, families, and the community as well as providing consultative services to others. Ashley is currently in her second year of her graduate program and has started practicum in the schools, she will begin her first internship in the fall of 2016.

Biography of DeShae Davis

DeShae Davis is a doctoral candidate in the SFASU School Psychology Program from Houston, Texas. Psychology has been a part of DeShae's life indirectly for many years. From childhood, DeShae has always been fascinated by human behavior and understanding how the mind works. She received her B.S. in Psychology from Stephen F. Austin State University in 2007. Her research experiences and interests vary across several domain including applied behavior analysis, psychometrics,

social skills intervention for individuals with special needs, eyewitness

testimony, body image, implicit and explicit prejudices, complex trauma, obesity, and social media. DeShae's personal research examines racial and ethnic microaggressions and cognitive complexity on the construct of differentiation of self. As a result of her involvement in research, DeShae has had opportunities to present at several conferences hosted by the Southwestern Psychological Association, Texas Association of School Psychologists, and the Association of Black Psychologist, Office of Multicultural Affairs (SFASU), and East Texas' Area Health Education Center. In addition to conducting research, DeShae works as a student clinician in the School Psychology Assessment Center (SPAC), a clinical resource of the SFASU campus and community. DeShae also has supervised experiences in intervention, behavior management, and consultation of individuals representing a wide range of ages, populations, and needs through her work with several school districts. Upon completion of her Doctorate in School Psychology, DeShae aspires to obtain her Licensure as a Psychologist and commit her professional energy to building connections between scholarship and practice.

Biography of Aubrey McKenzie

Aubrey McKenzie As a budding adolescent raised in poverty, abuse, and abandonment, even as a child Aubrey knew that she had to be of service to others. After becoming a teenage mother and temporarily losing focus her own passion, she worked in customer service and hospitality before re-entering the world of academia. In her senior year as an undergraduate she began
researching for her first conference centered around Gender, Sex, and Power added fuel to the fire of her passion for people and the understanding of cultures and how they can affect ones life. This insight has given her the ability to sincerely communicate with individuals from many cultures. It has also given her the opportunity to help individuals understand a culture other than their own. Moreover, her work has helped others understand their own culture. Cultural competence was merely a catalyst to understanding heterogeneity and
as a Court Appointed Special Advocate this has given her the strength and tenacity to be a liaison for persons who otherwise would not be heard. As an employer for the Medically Dependent Children's program she fights for the safety and care of persons who are vulnerable and cannot fight for themselves. Her job is giving others hope no matter if she is speaking to a child who was orphaned or a young adult who has lost sight of their dreams. She reminds them that they can be happy, can be heard, are worthy, have the right to live, and the right to be free. She does this work wholeheartedly, as she walks through graduate school as a single mother, a woman of color, an employer and an employee in the field of Humanities spreading what she has learned while continuing to learn from those around.

Biography of Juliet Aura

Juliet Aura is a first year International Doctoral student from Nairobi Kenya enrolled in the Stephen F. Austin State University School Psychology Program. This is her first time to visit the United States and is excited to be in the program. She joined the program in the fall of 2015 after working for 3 years in the corporate sector back in her home country in corporate training. Juliet is also a certified Human Resource practioner. Psychology has always been an area of interest for Juliet and changing from the corporate field to School Psychology was an opportunity for her to get to learn more and grow in the field. She intends to use the knowledge and skills learned from the program to help children with various issues in the schools by implementing both system level interventions and interventions customized to individual needs. Juliet believes that mental health is important in society and if you start with the children, society will progress as a whole. In the future, Juliet hopes to extend her services beyond the borders of the United States to schools back at home where she plans to work in conjunction with the government and non- profit organizations to extend the much needed services of school psychologists. Juliet is currently involved in various project with her professors and is looking forward to an exciting time in the school psychology field.

Yaisa Mann

Body Image Expert, Professional Hype Girl and CEO of SwagHER Fitness

Chapter 2

LOVING THE SKIN I'M IN
by Yaisa Mann

"Mirror, mirror on the wall, who is the fairest one of them all?" Not only is this question from the fairytale, "Snow White and the Seven Dwarfs", but it is also the question that many girls ask themselves. My own self-hatred was magnified when I dated a guy named Jason during undergrad in college. He was a member of the fraternity, Kappa Alpha Psi, better known as the Kappas or pretty boys. At the time, I had just pledged into Delta Sigma Theta Sorority, Inc., and was new to this college sub-culture. I felt that I had arrived. I had paid my dues by "making good grades," staying focused, and studying. I didn't have a reputation for being promiscuous, which seemed to be the "thing to do". I had a part-time campus job and was able to pay my own bills. We had the ideal campus relationship; my sorority letters were crimson and cream and matched his Kappa colors.

Midway through our relationship, coming back from the Island Water Park my boyfriend Jason told me that I wasn't his ideal type because he usually dated light-skinned girls.

> In his exact words, he said, while looking up at me, "It's funny who you end up dating when you're used to dating light-skinned girls."

The sharply articulated syllables rolled off his tongue as if he were pronouncing a bad word.

I held my palm up toward him and snickered. "I guess I'm not your type." Then I felt stupid for asking his likes and dislikes because I didn't get the answer that I wanted. I wanted to remind him that he was my same color, but didn't think that that reminder would change the situation.

"Hey, what's that look for? Look, if I offended you, I was just telling you the truth. Sorry."

My mind raced as I quickly regrouped in the face of my painful loss of round one. "Oh, you don't have to apologize for showing your true colors."

"Meaning?" he asked.

There was a long pause before I spoke. "Can we say ... insensitive?" I said, as I shot him a sarcastic frown.

"The way I feel doesn't take away from the fact that I like you," he said as if giving me some type of peace offering.

I hunched up my shoulders and shook my head and remained quiet for the remainder of our drive home.

From his seat he couldn't see the expression on my face—half outraged, half saddened. My feelings were hurt and I soon lost my appetite for food and for him. He just sat there in the driver's seat enjoying the music, letting the sun dance over our heads, as we passed under the tall palms. I wanted to tell him to let the top up on his convertible so as to lessen my basting in the 107-degree heat. As I stared out of my window, I couldn't help catching glimpses of myself in the mirror. I studied my face, noticing the Fresno, California heat had toasted my surrendering complexion from honey brown to medium chestnut brown.

I remember asking the Kappa about his ideal female because a part of me thought that he wanted a light-skinned girlfriend. I brought up the topic because I had noticed that most of the Kappas dated Black girls with light skin. I didn't consider my skin as light and felt insecure compared to light-skinned girls. He answered that he liked light skin girls and that I was one of the darkest girls that he had ever dated. Even though he didn't call me ugly or less than perfect, I felt that I wasn't good enough. Looking back, I would've skipped that discussion because he never gave me any reason to feel unsure about his interest in me. But back then, I was still new to the dating game and was still dealing with my own insecurities growing up as a black girl.

Having beautiful skin was important. I felt that I was no competition for any of the other females and that I was a stand-in girlfriend.

From my experiences, black guys had a lot of ego, and always wanted a girl who was a "trophy," model type, which meant light skin, long hair, and a perfect thin yet curvy body. They wanted to have the best girl and wanted all of their friends and other peers to lust after her. Ultimately, I felt that I would not have any security in this relationship based on my skin color. This affected my thinking and how I perceived the world and myself because dating was the quintessential college experience that would eventually lead up to marriage. I felt that light skinned girls were the standard of beauty and I would have to compete with them.

From what I saw at the Greek parties and on the campus "yard" most other Kappas had light skinned girlfriends. Such was the case when the Kappa and I first started dating, he asked me to go to his fraternity ball. I was excited and planned to look my best. However, when the evening finally came, the majority of the Kappas' dates were all light skinned with long hair. As I sat at the table, I looked around at all of the brothers and most of them were dark skinned.

Since I had always been called brown-skinned, I compared my status to a certain part of an old time chant, "If you're white you're all right. Nowadays being white and all right means being light skinned. If you're brown, stick around. If you're black, get back." Being brown was safe but being "barely brown" felt like standby status until the "real" thing came.

Years later I have moved on from that experience, yet I realize my feelings during that ride home were a product of my own personal history and experiences. I realized that I was just as "color struck" as he was, but I had never claimed it.

Growing up my parents never discussed what it meant to be black, but I was always racially aware and experienced the effects of it. In the 80's during my elementary days, I grew up in Armona, California located in the San Joaquin Valley. The neighborhood was mostly white. Whiteness affected the way I viewed and represented myself. For the most part, I always tried to fit in with others and felt that there was no place for me to be a black girl. Some examples included not talking about the music I listened to, like Janet Jackson because everyone in my friendship group liked Madonna, Tiffany Gibson and Cindy Lauper. Another example was not sharing the latest dances that I knew because it was expected that I could dance. From this perspective, I began to minimize my blackness as a means of avoiding being at the center of attention. In most cases getting attention among my friends would mean having to represent my race and there were always questions. My skin and hair were always scrutinized. What kind of hair grease do you use? Is it cooking grease? Do you wash your hair? Why does your hair smell like cocoa butter? When I hung around the few black girls at the school it was common for us to compare and contrast our skin and hair to one another. We would roll up our sleeves and line our arms up side by side to see who was the lightest. Another test was through our hair; we always stretched out our ponytails to see who had the longest hair. I wore my hair in ponytails adorned with knockers and barrettes. My hair was thick and frizzy with crinkly tight waves.

In the fifth grade, I began to idealize "so-called" white hair. My friends Jamie and Larissa always talked about how much Aqua Net hair spray they used on their hair. These cans came in fuchsia pink or turquoise blue, regular and super hold. Even though I didn't need hair spray, I wanted to spray my hair. I never touched my friends' hair, but I remember they had versatile styles, they could wear their hair in curly perms, blow-dried straight, and spiral curls curled with a curling iron or crimped with crimper. My mom still did my hair. They had the freedom to do their own hair. Sometimes I thought that their freedom made them more confident and pretty.

When my mother thought that I was ready for a relaxer, I went to the beauty shop. I was eleven years old. I remember going to the hair shop on a Saturday afternoon. I remember the process. It was a black hairdresser named Elise, but there was also a heavy-set white guy that worked there too. I think that it was his shop. The beautician applied a thick white creamy paste to my hair roots that smelled like ammonia, bleach, acid, and something that could singe my nose hairs. The relaxer was left on my hair for about five to seven minutes. Then the beautician shampooed my hair for a few minutes to make sure the chemicals were completely out of my hair. When the beautician finished the last wash, she combed through my hair with her claw-like fingers and said "Silky, silk. Now you have white girl hair". Anyway, once my hair had been relaxed, blow-dried, and curled when the beautician turned me around in the chair to face the big mirror I was shocked. My hair looked like my friends. My crinkly hair was silky straight and shiny and all the way down my back. I remember the hairdresser saying that I looked Indian. I had never seen an Indian or their hair, but I imagined that being a compliment. This was my first compliment. I had never gotten compliments about my hair. I felt like a Black doll.

After getting my hair relaxed, keeping it straight was another process. I remember the first time I sat in the kitchen chair to get my hair pressed. My mother put the hot-comb on the stove and let the iron get hot. As I sat in the chair, I watched the smoke coming from my thinned hair, as my mother would comb through it. The smell of burnt hair would fill the kitchen, but it was all in the name of attaining "good" hair. I knew the difference between "good" and "bad" hair. "Good" hair flowed and was silky, smooth, shiny, and blonde. It blew around lively in the wind and then fell back into place perfectly. For most black girls, and me this hair was a fantasy. "Bad" hair was kinky. It was nappy and hard to comb through. I learned from television, through Dark and Lovely relaxer commercials, that natural hair in the form and texture of an Afro was African (bad) and that Barbie was ideal. Throughout my childhood when white girls wanted to play in my hair, I would tense up, knowing good and well that my mom had invested too much into my hair by braiding, twisting, pressing and greasing to let them mess it up.

Even though my mother told me not to apply heat to my hair every day, I wanted to be like my white friends. I treated my hair like my friends did theirs. Every day I blow dried, curling ironed and hair sprayed it with Aqua Net. Eventually over time, my hair became damaged, brittle, and fell out. My hair was short. I never complained to my mother but she had a plan to resuscitate my hair. She took me to another shop and paid for me to get a "wave nouveau". This was a new kind of jerry curl that had added softness and a looser curl than a "jherri curl" did. Before the hairdresser could apply the product and hair rolling rods, she had to cut off the damaged long end strands and make my hair even all over. I felt bald headed. To be honest, I felt like a boy. I somehow managed to find stylish ways to fix my hair. I always had a style with big bangs and the rest of my hair was pulled back in a ponytail.

After about year of having short hair my mother took me to get my first hair weave. I was fourteen years old. Instead of going to the shop, I went to someone's house. I don't know where my mom bought the hair from or how she knew what color to get to match my hair. The hair was called Italian Silky Straight and was fourteen inches long. Nene was well known in town for "hooking some weave up". Instead of a "full-head weave" I only got tracks sewn into the back of my hair. My hair was the same length of my hair when I first got it relaxed. I felt safe. I began to like myself. I felt that I had a new start at having long hair.

My experience wearing hair weave gave me a range of emotions. In high school, I had abandoned all of my white friends and hung out with all blacks. Most of my black friends wore hair braid extensions or ponytails that were also synthetic hair. I was one of the few Black girls who wore hair weave. The other girls who wore hair weave kept it short, whereas mines was halfway down my back. Some of the girls thought that it was my hair. I was always careful about making sure that none of my weave tracks were showing. But most of them knew that I wore hair weave extensions and would ask me a range of questions such as: Why do you wear that weave? or How long is your real hair? And some would flat out tell me that "I wasn't all that," meaning that I wasn't better than them even if my hair was longer than theirs. Some even went as far by saying; give the horse his hair back. It wasn't the questions or even the "hating" by suggesting that I was wearing horse hair that bothered me the most, it was the attitude they had toward me. However, my experience was different with black guys. They never seemed to care and I actually became more popular for having longer hair compared to most black girls having shorter hair. Every time my hair weave became an issue, I felt that my security was being taken away. My hair weave covered the fact that I had damaged my hair. Even though the hair wasn't mine, having hair was more realistic than having short hair.

In addition to all of the changes with my hair, my mother began buying bleaching cream. I remember the bleaching cream jar saying that the cream would lighten dark pigment in the skin, and that it contained a sunscreen to prevent darker skin from reoccurring. I thought that my brown skin would eventually transform to a light skinned glow like singer and former Miss America Vanessa Williams. But I stayed brown. I would ritually cake the bleaching cream on my face before I went to bed. I thought that the more I used, the more I would lighten up. And that maybe one morning I would wake up and have my brown skin disappear. My mother would often question if I'd used the cream. "Let me see your face?" She would ask. Then she would gently grip my chin and have me profile from left to right.

"See, it's taken away some of my dark spots." I remember answering her first time she asked me. I wanted her to not only see my scars vanished, but my brown skin too. Sometimes I wanted to ask her why she wanted me to use "this" cream, because her motherly measures were intercepted by my own thoughts of becoming something else. Like most black girls, it was an ever-present source of anxiety to prove I was good enough and beautiful. Since I wasn't getting the results she wanted, I bought a bar of Ambi lightening complexion soap to ensure my chances of getting lighter.

When I went to cheerleader camp at UC Davis during my senior year of high school there was no way of avoiding the sun. The situation only got darker. I was the only black cheerleader on my high school squad; mind you there were about fifty of us ranging from freshman, junior varsity, and varsity. I only saw ten other black girls, total, from other schools. All of the cheer workshop clinics began at 8:00am and the sun was always there to greet me. After each day ended I would head to the dorm bathroom to wash my face with my Ambi soap. My face was always tender and blistered and then I would ice on layers of bleaching cream. For me to achieve the beauty standard, I went through the motions. Despite the fact that my arms and legs blackened, my face only mattered.

After camp was over I knew that cheerleading wasn't for a black girl like me. Although I learned many spirit chants and cheers, the only thing I remembered was that I wasn't excited about being the only black cheerleader from my high school. Everything about cheerleading seemed to be based on white culture. White girls loved to be in the sun, they wanted tanned skin. In addition, having long hair was important. Cheerleaders wore their hair in big ponytails and when they wore their hair down, they loved to swing it. Since I wore hair weave, I was limited on hairstyles. I had to be careful not to show where my hair weave had been sewn into my scalp. I couldn't put my hair in a ponytail. Back then, nothing could compare to their free moving silky hair, as well as the privilege of swimming and I guess sun bathing and tanning. The isolation of my black experience left me open to further internalizing my own color complex.

> PLAINLY SAID, I WAS ALWAYS COMPARING MYSELF TO THE BEAUTY STANDARDS OF WHITENESS. WHITENESS WAS INEVITABLE, EVEN WHEN HANGING WITH MY FEW BLACK FRIENDS. MOST OF MY BLACK FRIENDS WORE THEIR HAIR BRAIDED WITH EXTENSIONS AND ALSO HATED BEING IN THE SUN.

My mother's idea of helping me achieve beauty involved introducing me into a world of skin bleach, hair straighteners, and extensions. My mother raised me to believe that light skin and long hair were beautiful. I never felt pressured by my mother; I actually liked the idea of having longer hair and lighter skin. Later I learned that my grandfather disapproved of my father marrying my mother because she wasn't a Louisiana Creole, but mainly because she wasn't "light" enough and didn't have "good" hair. This was my mother's experience and in my mind the reason why she made sure that my skin was bleached and my hair straightened. Even though skin bleach and hair straighteners were new to me, the color complex is not new to African Americans and the root of the problem reaches back to slavery and continued after they were free.

After I graduated from high school, outside of my family, on my own, I saw sorority life as a way to connect with a progressive black culture on my college campus at California State University, Fresno. Sorority sisters wore Greek paraphernalia, jackets adorned with big numbers on the back and with names like Un-fade-able, Treacher-ACE, Red Rum (pronounced murder spelled backwards). At noontime the Greeks "ran the yard" and filled the free speech area, the outside food court where they socialized. They advertised their events in this space, promoting their weekend parties by performing "yard shows" by stepping and chanting songs about being Greek.

They were not limited to the free speech area, where they hung out during lunchtime, but in the Satellite auditorium is where they took center stage and during the spring they "stepped" against other Greeks on campus and from other California schools at the step show. As a freshman and new to this environment, I was amazed. Altogether there are four NPHC (National Pan Hellenic) sororities, Alpha Kappa Alpha, Delta Sigma Theta, Zeta Phi Beta, and Sigma Gamma Rho. Among these groups from my perspective only two stood out the most. The ladies of Delta Sigma Theta Sorority, Inc, known as the "Delta's" stepped hard and were always memorable. They varied their outfit style, which could range from army fatigues and military boots to business suits and stilettos. Their colors were officially crimson and cream, but usually substituted them with red and white. Even as an outsider, I was aware of the Delta's biggest rival were the AKA's (Alpha Kappa Alpha's). Their colors were pink and green and they were really prissy and used hand-held mirrors during their step performances and dances to look at themselves while they chanted with soft voices and ended their routines with their "skee-wee" call, in a high-pitched screech. From my freshman perspective these two sororities represented two sides of womanhood, one that told you to notice her, and that she wasn't afraid to get down, while the other was more delicate and exhibited traditional femininity.

As an outsider, on my own I recognized that the AKA's were mainly lighter skinned girls with long hair with a more pretentious attitude denoting upper class status quiet mannerisms. Among the Delta's there was a mixture of girl types—dark, light, and brown with varying hairstyles and lengths. From my outside status they didn't appear to hide behind status, they were confident and direct meaning they just handled their business. Observing these groups, I began to carefully observe them and critique myself wanting to know which group I best fit in. Pledging into a sorority was a common rite of a passage for many Black college students. For example, a person would ask if you were going to pledge and then they would say, you look like a Delta or an AKA. Stereotypes for Delta's were usually characterized as outspoken and independent. Unlike the Delta's personality traits, the AKA's stereotypes were mainly based on appearance. If a girl had light skin and colored eyes that were light brown, green, or blue, it was assumed that she would become and AKA. Based on this, I was curious what other people thought I looked like. Even though the Delta's were all that, I felt that the AKA's represented the quintessential sorority girl and had the Mrs. Degree status.

I pledged Delta. They were the beauty, body image, and self esteem on campus. And true enough; once I became a Delta, I developed a newfound confidence. I had "sisters" who I was now connected with through our sorority letters, community service and hard stepping routines. I felt that I became more popular because I was more visible on campus and was involved in more activities. However, this life had its ups and downs. With all of my sisters and newfound confidence, deep down inside I was still insecure about my skin color; I still wore hair weave extensions and struggled with wondering if I was pretty enough for my Kappa boyfriend.

College could only take me so far from the lessons that I learned as a girl. My parents and family members would caution my cousins and I not to play in the sun. My mom would always say, "Do you want to get black?" At the time I didn't care; I just wanted to play. Blackness was taboo. Both of my parents drank coffee and I, too, wanted to try some. However, one of my friends said that coffee would make me black. So, I needed to stay away from it. She recommended that I stick to hot chocolate. At such a young age, I had no idea that events like these would later haunt me, but I was being taught that light skin was apparently more beautiful than dark skin.

As an undergrad I majored in English and African American Studies. For my Master's thesis I wrote about the color complex. On my first attempt to finish my PhD I wrote my dissertation on how black girls like me spent our lives pretending, never learning how to love ourselves or how to be loved by others. My research revealed that black girls choose to conform because black culture encourages this behavior. We are rewarded greatly. The behavior and values give us status within our communities. Yet not all black girls accept this idea. There are black girls and girls of all races who are confident and not concerned about how others may perceive them. They are aware of the negative lessons and incentives. Regardless of how they measure up, they are confident. These girls express their feelings and make positive choices. Just as I have learned lessons from family and friends, I have also learned that "beauty comes from being yourself," best said by Coco Chanel.

Biography of Yaisa Mann

Body Image Expert, Professional Hype Girl and CEO of SwagHER Fitness, LLC and Pigeon Toed Publishing, LLC Yaisa Mann is leading the way blending body image, fun, positivity, and motivation to empower girls and women.

She has years of academic teaching and research experience holding a dual B.A. in English and African American Studies from California State University, Fresno; M.A. in English from her alma mater, and on her journey to completing a PhD in Interdisciplinary Studies from the University of Oklahoma. She holds countless fitness certifications: YMCA Group Fitness Certification, Healthy Lifestyle Wellness Coach Certification, YASA (YMCA Aquatic Safety Assistant) Certification and is licensed to teach Zumba Basic 1, Zumba Basic 2, Zumba Toning, Aqua Zumba, Zumba Kids, Zumba Gold, Zumba Sentao, R.I.P.P.E.D., Turbo Kick, Hip Hop Hustle, and Bokwa just to name some of the hottest workout trends.

Yaisa not only follows the trends but also makes up her own! She created and taught the first course in body image ever taught at the University of Oklahoma in 2008 starting with the course Body Image versus Reality: Popular Culture and the Beauty Myth; she was selected to be featured in the 40th Anniversary Edition of Our Bodies, Ourselves (2011); was selected to be featured in the National Eating Disorders Association Awareness Month Calendar Campaign (2013) for her body image advocacy; was selected to be a speaker for the Great Night of the Orators at the University of Oklahoma (2013); won the University of Oklahoma Inaugural Brightest Idea Speaker Symposium Contest (2013), invited to serve as a board member for the Oklahoma Eating Disorders Association (2014), and was recently invited to the Dillard's pace setters winner's circle as a beauty advisor for Kiehl's (2016).

Her interest in body image and fitness came directly out of her own personal experiences with her brown skin color, curly and frizzy hair texture with lots of shrinkage, junk food binge eating, battle with maintaining a healthy weight and overall struggle with self-acceptance and being who God made her to be. Although she has struggled to see her own beauty feeling the pressure from cultural influences like the color complex and media pressures, she has always felt empowered and free to live by her own rules through dance.

Her passion for dance inspired her to start her own women's wellness SwagHER Fitness. In order to promote a healthy self esteem and body image in girls and women SwagHER Fitness incorporates popular and effective workouts like Zumba, boot camp, aqua fitness, hip hop, and (online and face-to-face) personal and group coaching. Yaisa can be booked for your next big event that needs an energizer through fitness, motivational speaking or a healthy dose of a body image seminar! She invites you to start loving your body by living by your own rules!

A California native, Yaisa currently resides in the Norman, OK with her family. Her children Jalen, Josiah, and Jael are her inspiration and her joy.

Contact information: Yaisa Mann
Phone: 405.473.1566
Email: yaisa@swagherfitness.com
Website: www.swagherfitness.com

Follow SwagHER Fitness on Facebook, Twitter, Instagram, Snapchat, and YouTube

Candace Liger

CEO of The Liger Company

Chapter 3

BE YOU

by Candace Liger

When I was four
I taught myself how to eat the entire world
It took me until six
to find out what flavor the Mississippi
Delta wind was.
And much like any place in the south,
the aroma was intoxicating of dead bodies
and busy bibles.

My father
a man with branches for arms
poetry as magnolia flowers
and roots forming his insecurities
Taught me early
that leaving home
wasn't as hard as biting his own bark

He wrote poetry.
simple and humble,
And every Valentine's day
I would receive his love written
on grains of murdered bark
shiny enough
to reflect my scars.

With age, the poetry became alive.
With age, he became closer to death.

I became closer to a cannibal
because I only felt him when I tasted
myself and eventually
it became to hard to digest.

My scars
My scars were displaced in soil
Love bled in and out of our lesions
We all Learned to use knives to cut away pain
And when daddy's poetry became nothing
more than an unintended drunk stagger
I mutilated the memory on my body.

At 13, I stopped writing
Never for lack of inspiration
Maybe a lack of desire to convert another storybook
into a riddle

I watched in silence
I watched his body eat its own existence
Never using his mouth
Always using scars past down from generations of dystrophy and disease
Some say that some old lady placed on root on his grandfather
That passed down
And plagued every child with illness
and creativity

I didn't take long for me to notice
how quiet the world became
To someone who wasn't finely broken like the soil
The poetry became further from a-b-a-b rhyme scheme
to a bootlegged self-fulfilled holocaust
bled into silence

By 18, I lost my virginity on the fourth of July to man who never heard
a woman scream
I blame that on my legs
Because whatever voice I was a bandage over his ego
But Between his fireworks and my daddy's wheelchair I can't recall
which one
protested God's calculation of physics

I didn't want to remember he existed.
He, barely breathing and muffled in voice, tried desperately to force
the sounds from his throat into a poem
But all I could ever hear was the sound of his inferior genetic makeup

And these scars
These scars aren't a testimony of rebellion
but rather what's left of years of closed eyes
And misunderstood looks
But never a question
loud enough for me to answer

My scars lay on his deathbed and before I could kiss his forehead
I couldn't help but think
that if my scars reflected his
would I too have lonely drifting from my eyes
paralyzed completely in some stranger's house
Would I be sensitive to the heat of the sun
Would my voice be strong enough to whisper
"I love you" into my own daughter's ear
Or would I be forced to eat myself whole
Until I was vegetated and
still hungry

I prayed death to him.
My soul could no longer hold his deterioration of body
Though his mind was in tact
I missed his poetry and his words
I missed his height
And his weight
And his voice.

Tell me that you see my scars
And the pieces leftover from them.

I'll write my poetry..
type it loudly on keyboards
Just to make noise
Recreating any sound like
I once heard from my father's woodwork
Sometimes with my eyes closed
hoping I would see him on Valentine's day
when love knew no funny gestures
or no awkward shifts in conversation

When world didn't look so much like one needle,

and a million bleeding wounds

When I was flawless.

And I guess that was when you were too.

For now, we all should feel lucky.
Our bodies can still hold all the pieces leftover
from planets crashing into space.

Lucky
We have legs
We only have scars
And a voice
If you want to know how I got mine

open your throat
and ask me.

For as long as I can remember, my body has been a sort of sacrificial entity that I submitted into the universe. I've felt as if it didn't belong to me, or as if I was experiencing my life in a 3rd person world. In moments, few and far in between, I've felt superhuman; like I could manage to create a rip in time's fabric large enough to hide all the skeletons that made home in my mind. I understood early growing up in the Mississippi Delta that my dark skin and athletic build was a common sight in the community population. For some reason however, scars on my hands and the thickness of my legs was the framework of much ridicule. I remember how I got the scars; I have not reached the place to speak of it.

> I WAS THICKY THICK GUL. WITHOUT A SHADOW OF A DOUBT. CORNBREAD AND LIMA BEAN EATING THANG. AND THE SCARS HAD BEEN THERE AS LONG AS I REMEMBER. I LEARNED HOW TO MANEUVER MY BODY TO HIDE THEM, BUT I COULDN'T ESCAPE THE FATE OF EXPOSURE.

We all played outside, me and my other dark athletic friends, drank the baggie kool-aid pickle juice residual, and enjoyed freedom--in the only flavor we have ever known. I had no idea what sunburn felt like back then. (side note: the first time I felt sunburn in Oklahoma after getting in the shower, I thought I was dying) I remember being happy and sad. I remember belonging and longing for solitude. The battle was cyclical and I was a planet that lost its orbit early on. It reflected mostly in my isolation, not in my social aptitude.

My dark skin narrated the wounds of my esteem throughout elementary school. My scars told the story out loud, without my permission. I remember bracing myself for the pain. Pain became practiced.

"Oil Spill" and "tar baby" were by far some of the most dehumanizing terms ever shoved into my face; they came from black boys. One black boy in particular named "Pug" (named because of plug that extended from the back of his head reminiscent of an electrical socket) would torment my life by calling me the most heinous names the dictionary refused to define. He was a little taller than me at the time, tootsie roll colored skin with tight snake eyes; he was actually cute, if my memory doesn't fail me. Anyway, I used to become so furious at his taunting that I would threaten to hit him if he didn't stop. I never really instigated it because I understood the level of crazy this brotha possessed. He was a young misogynist with no damn home training, let my momma tell it.

A funny thing about storytelling--as you become older, the stories equip themselves with an illusion of fantasy and removal. When Yaisa Mann invited me into this project to tell my story, I had no clue of which part of my past has directly affected my views on body image. Never could I have been prepared to unfile these stories--especially the one of Pug.

Walking back into the building after either a fire drill or from recess, I remember Pug shoving me in my back. It caused enough momentum to lunge my body forward and forced me to quickly catch my footing before I made impact with the ground. The crowd of students saw me struggle and shifted their attention to the potential of a good

fried chicken and hog meat kinda brawl.
I turned around and pushed him back. I didn't stay to see what happened to him, so I walked smooth off---breathing calmness into my crinkled up forehead. I looked up to see the "Hayes Cooper Magnet School" sign and wondered how this fool ever passed the test to get in. All of a sudden I heard my name.

"Candace!", he says calmly behind me as I walked off.

In an agitated spin, I turned around to lock eyes on this punk. Before I could get rotated enough to see his face--the sole of shoe was coming 3 million mph towards my face. The next thing I remember was looking up at a crowd of people, some laughing and some wincing. My friends helped me up and the teacher ordered the chatter to resume silently through the hallways. Pug's face disappeared into the school doors. He was smiling. Meanwhile, the swelling pulsated its way to the surface of my right eye.

This was the first time where the disgust of my physical presence drove someone so mad their only choice was to resort to physical force. This was the first time I remember a boy hitting me and being proud about it at the same time. This was the first time I ever questioned if my body would be a war zone for the inevitable tragedy that so many women encounter in their lifetimes. This was the first time I realized that friends may not come forward in the midst of turmoil. I saw the looks the people gave me--both of pity and negligence. Although hands reached out to help me out, they had never reached out to stop the insanity of Pug.

I have a horrible memory of my childhood--only a select few moments shattered throughout my brain in fleeting reminders. I blame it on the softball that hit me square in the face, breaking my nose, in 2002. But this moment, disturbed me. I thought I was beautiful and intelligent. I thought I was athletic and inspiring. I didn't think those qualities would serve as a threat and my body would be offered as sacrifice.

be YOUtiful

As time went on, Pug did grow fond of me and he regretted the moment where pain was the only flattery he could muster for me. He apologized while I became a band aid. Pain shifted my idea of what my body could handle, and if my body was worthy of expected of moral behavior.

When I got pregnant with my son in the early part of 2007, the first thought that came to my mind was, "How will I hold him?" My imagination created the images of all the pictures of me uncomfortably gripping my child, scars in perfect position, attempting to look motherly while battling a disconnection that was void of known solution.

I had been in labor for 18 hours in an attempt to have a natural delivery at Integris Baptist Hospital. My doctor encouraged induction, so I arrived to the hospital unaware that I had already began to have contractions. I had planned on turning down the induction anyway, so it played out nicely. My sweat steamed the pale walls and reverberated itself onto the forehead of my mother who was all familiar with how life enters into the world. After a tiresome bout of grunts, nurses suggested that my heart rate and baby's heart rate had increased exponentially--only to be saved by a cesarean.

My mom had to hold me still as the anesthesiologist shattered his needle into my spine with a force surpassing the pain of the labor. Minus catching a glimpse of what my organs look like (and how they can never possibly put that stuff in back correctly), I don't remember much.

I woke up in a cold room with the feeling that I had been abducted by aliens---it was just the smell of the room that gave the illusion of extraterrestrially. My door slowly crept open coupled with a knock that suggested, "Whatever you say, I am gonna come in anyway". In her arms, was the white and blue striped baby blankets they assign to every newborn.

The first touch of my son was natural because I knew him already. In

www.beyoutifulbooks.com

the first moment, I forgot the amount of pain I had just endured the previous hours. I didn't think of Pug, or any other person who had made my body feel less than perfect. I didn't think of the scar now protruding from my lower abdomen. I didn't think of my scars. Still high on the meds, I almost had no idea why they were handing me the child.

> BUT WHEN I HELD HIM, LOOKED AT HIM, IN THAT MOMENT, PAIN BECAME A CONCEPT NOT YET STUDIED IN SCHOOL. I WAS PERFECT IN MY EMBRACE AND HE WAS PERFECT IN HIS EXISTENCE. I HAD OPTED TO HAVE HIM STAY WITH ME VERSUS IN THE BABY GREENHOUSE.

Ode to Mother. Nature

For you
Mother of ages
Prophetic Genius grasping
root to world

I've seen your face hidden
in my hallucinations

I measured your
witchcraft meticulously

See we, vibrate penetrating
frequencies

I've Felt your wet sun kiss
against my
humid Mississippi skin

and your taste
of starseeds and venus

Your stillness is immovable
Your quiet explodes the cosmos

And this place

this concrete jungle
arranges our thinking
to damn near infertile

But you dare leave me withered.

Saw your breeze pick up
the broken pieces of
my heart
and made them
dance in your wind song

Your blood taps my umbrella different tunes of patience
Your scent lingers in my promises

And you
being mother nature and all
Unspoken
and Lovely
speaking volumes
Like how you do that trick
that makes women's
periods synchronize without their consent
or consciousness

I thought I'd give up on you
and myself
And break open and
scattered like building blocks
on
hardwood floors
Or the knees

that never found out
how
to kneel down and pray

You designed this body
crashed riptide warrior
sunken
between this pressure reducing
bariatric mattress and
peaceful purgatory
you purposefully
designed for moments like these

In this place
drowned brightly in
artificial lighting and latex
allergies

I crashed moans to mapless
destinations on
walls
500 heartbeats
500 missed calls
You intertwined my vulnerability
with your mayhem of acid rain

And I've never been so in love
with pain in my life.

contraction

I forgot how to breathe
or whether if it was my uterus,
lungs or both that was suppose
to know how to

the beads of my sweat

clenched tight
to the nape of my neck
to the night of my skin
And then another

Contraction

each gasp
that I inhaled
became an entity within
itself
And somewhere between
the pacific ocean and this morning
You made me metaphysical

Contraction

I made each breath
your breath..
each movement
an earthquake..

And every vibration of my
voice trickled
its way through our instinctual
ability to love and fight

Contraction
And I have never
Ever
Been so in love with pain
in my life.

Contraction.

I damn near thought I was gonna die.
Push.

It's really possible that I did
Push.
Cause for the first time
I saw God
when I saw you and knew
that when you created
a woman's womb
you had crafted a threshold
to the supernatural

Push

And my mind began to draw
letters around your cumulus cloud
The ring around your orange moon

Dear Seeds,

I don't want to push you away
germinated and exposed
into the woes of
this dynasty
I want to push you into phenomenal.
Push
I want to push you into
my chest and smell
your curly petals as they
tickle my nose
Push.
Help you get up from
your first broken
stem to stand on the roots of your toes
Push.
Watch your daydreams go from proportional
to scalene and finally
your magnum opus
Push

be YOUtiful

I decorated my pain
regal adornments
warrior queen
Our pain
and scars
understood ideologies of astrology
Libra symmetry, Scorpio goddess
Moon in Taurus

Our pain
uttered from these dry, brittle lips
was so electric
my genetics aggressively connected
polar charges until
lightning bolts ran from my palms
your fathers

And this pain
This wonderful pain
This pain was OUR pain
Antiquated, ferocious, and buoyant

I pray you omnipotent
I pray you have the
belly of Nut,
the eyes of a crystal ball
the fearlessness of Bantu
the appetite of your father,
the spirit of Assata,
the truth of Ma'at,
the wonders of Alice,
the magic of a Liger,
the spine of a giant,
the wisdom of forever
the heart of each one of your mothers...
and that you never have to compromise

www.beyoutifulbooks.com

one for the other.

I pray you peaceful in knowing
that you being you
is a blanket to the wind
Because mother nature can seem so cold sometimes
I pray that you never
have to understand
that line.

And in my last
pushes
Mother Nature
in the moment, where I thought I would give up
Be at full bloom, black, and
beautiful

I saw you mother of ages
in the eyes of my babies
and i whispered in your`ear..
My God.

Pain, especially pain rooted in purpose and self-worth, can transform itself a million different ways. As a mother, the concept of body image lingers within the beautiful battle wounds. The pain we experience I do not believe is part of our fate. I could deduce an experience to a reminder of how strong I am to survive. The reality, I believe, is negative experiences prepare us for pain. How we handle the pain can ultimately shape the self-confidence we exude when nobody's watching.

As fitness coach and trainer, I am held to a higher expectation of health and wellness-often times minimizing my vantage point of body-image. So, when I would tell people that I suffered from anxiety and depression as a result the perception of appearance and experiences around my appearance, the response illustrates how ineffective my testimony, rather vulnerable or not, actually is. By comparison, I had been blessed to understand the root cause of my anxiety, and I spent many years tackling it directly. I suffered from heavy scarring on my hands that would debilitate my essences. I would tremble in close quarters to people. I would easily drop and mismanage anything small that may appear as fragile.

I didn't know how to hold my baby.

I knew how to fight.

Contrary to this awkwardness, I did know how to fight, and I spent most of my childhood fighting other people's battles. When Pug delivered the embarrassing kick that knocked me to the ground, I knew what my body was capable of. It had become a machine of war, taking the impact of pain being delivered at the expense of pride or esteem. I learned how to conceal my trauma in smiles and forgetfulness. I understood how to get up without looking as if I had fallen. My skin, my scars, this body became a symbol for resilience before I ever wanted it to be.

The history is deep where I'm from. The history is deep in my melanin. Throughout ages, black women's bodies were the dumping grounds for unwanted energies. Anger, frustration, misogyny, patriarchy, and ostracism found refuge in knowing black woman's smile was as fleeting as their responsibility to her happiness. This body is a cocoon for my actual nakedness. With age, I understand how deeply these scars we carry can penetrate.

I have chosen how to select the battles worth fighting.

To tie my lessons together, pain can manifest itself in our visions of self-worth. Looking in the mirror, aware of my vulnerabilities, I managed to maneuver throughout the days, microaggressioning out my pain in different forms. Overcoming the labor of my own self-image, I understood the necessity to become a part of a profession where I could fight for others by inspiring those that feel less-than-perfect to achieve their body image goals, whatever they may consists of. The only problem with being a fitness trainer is convincing my clients that they are already beautiful.

When my clients come to me, immediately they begin a slippery-slope of comparing their body to my own---from legs to arms and that most common--stomach. They say things like "Don't you see all this fat?" and "This is so gross" as they point to some random area on their body, pinch the skin, and pull it out away from their bones to show me. They show me their scars; scars of womanhood, of neglect, of abuse, of shame; this is common. People manage to reverberate the very same negative rhetoric that has haunted them throughout their life as fact---as something to be shameful about. This punishment is self-inflicting and toxic--usually resulting in them realizing how much they would actually have to do to achieve the sometimes unreasonable goals they have set out for themselves. My first barrier to getting through to my clients is convincing them that they are already beautiful. It's almost as if the brain doesn't allow for the creation of positive self-investment any longer. They are their own Pug. That's a dangerous person to be.

I remember being a young girl looking in the mirror in awe of my beauty. The environment around my self-admiration was not relevant to my body image approval. My daughter Savahli, who is now 3 years old, does the same thing--except she takes it up a notch. She calls herself "cute" and "beautiful" and says it OUT LOUD; most importantly, she believes it. She listens to herself and allows her voice to vibrate in her own. At such a young age, she has embraced the power of mantra. And although she is my own seed, I can attest that her belief is conviction enough for me to believe.

Imagine if we all created a personal mantra that attested to our level of self-confidence. I would want any woman, who deems herself unworthy to be beautiful, to look in the mirror for a solid minute. In that minute, assess your face, your wrinkles, your ears, your hairline, your mouth. Each has a story of its own that needs to be told. Remember your pain; remember how you survived. Each square inch of your body is being pressed by 14.5lbs of atmospheric pressure.

be YOUtiful

> WE HAVE OVER A TON OF INVISIBLE ENERGY ENCOURAGING US TO COLLAPSE, TO BREAK, TO FALL UNDER THE PRESSURE. HOWEVER, WE DON'T REALIZE IT BECAUSE WE ARE SILENTLY RESILIENT, EVEN IN MOMENTS OF WEAKNESS. OUR BODY ARE MACHINES, CAPABLE OF WITHSTANDING THE PRESSURE SOCIAL INFLUENCE HAS ON OUR IDEALS. PUG AINT GOT NOTHING ON YOU. YOU JUST BELIEVE THAT.

Woman

Flawless, exceptional, righteous
supernova explosion of colors

Let your rainbow lead into
pots of your golden essence

Sheer elegance complementing your lovely curves that defy the hands of time

that could never fully grasp your beauty.

You have the timeless flutter of angels wings
that question

if God gave you away much too freely.

You are

A masterpiece woven in a world fashioned from your own womb.

You breathe fumes of resilience into your lungs daily.

Baby, Honey, Darling, or Sweetheart
will never do your name justice

Woman

The fabric clenched on your shape accentuate heartbreak and triumph.

www.beyoutifulbooks.com

The shoes on your feet have shared more rocky roads than Baskin Robbins

Your walk sways your hips giant pendulums of perfection.
And they say your clothes make you beautiful
Humpf

They must have never seen a woman broken into pieces birth compositions of springtime from her spirit

Sun kissed skin absorbing stardust and reflecting joy
from her smile

You tell them

Your lips are made for much more than fire engine red lipstick or kissing their neglected battle wounds.

You have learned to speak revivals into chaos.

Your legs
Your legs are built for much more than storefront silhouettes
or nair commercials.

You have learned to walk with grace while carrying buckets of everyone else's tears

For so long

Make the listen.
Make them hear your melodic song in their veins.

Let them know you know more than runway fashion.
You fashion precision with the stroke of your pen or the flick of your hand.

be YOUtiful

You are style, grace
Authentic and undeniably

a species endangered by media moguls and video vixens.

You are much more than some trendy hip hop fad gone wrong

Your diamond encrusted eyes are always in style.
Tell them
You are the framework of a galaxy.
The brilliance of philosophy.

The bass of your heartbeat guides the djembe into rhythm.
Your Queenly warsong has shattered the frequencies of tyrants.

You are the light and dark
North and South
Earth and Stars
All wrapped securely in the perfect little black dress.

Raise your head like the sunrise
Throw back your shoulders
and glide over murky waters
until your feet no longer understand the music of failure

Love
Like your hug could send chills down a zombie's spine

And when they ask you
How do you make it look so easy?
Tell them

It doesn't make sense to have it look hard
when you've practiced the perfection of
mother nature in the antiquity of your smile.

You are the reincarnation of what peace should feel like.

www.beyoutifulbooks.com

The epitome of what love should sound like

The instrumental of what heaven should look like

Your architecture has been worshipped like a deity.

Remember

Remember your spirit isn't easily broken like fake nails
You are the embodiment of
Nubia.

And
The messenger of life.

The world needs your style
to keep its cypher

complete.

Woman

You
are everything to everyone
every where

so wear yourself exquisite, impeccable
and most importantly

Wear your body, flawlessly.

Biography of Candace Liger

Candace Liger is the CEO of The Liger Company, focusing on art, activism, and wellness. Her current positions include Community Organizer for American Civil Liberties Union (ACLU), Executive Advisory Officer for the National Organization of Women OKC, certified health and wellness expert through her company #GoodFunk HeadQuarters, and an award-winning performance and spoken word artist. She is the founder of the Abstract Ebon Collective, a progressive media and event company that emphasizes creativity and social consciousness by incorporating a healing & racial justice lens to empower, educate, and inspire people of color.

As a facilitator for after school programming, she has worked with the Oklahoma City Urban League as a Peak Certified Instructor teaching spoken word and expressive movement and the lead Fitness Instructor at Langston University OKC JUMP Youth Program for 3 years.

Candace is the creator of a multitude of wellness offerings including JahRation Nation Dance Fitness - a dancehall and reggae based fitness class focusing on cardio training, weight loss, and muscle toning. As an online fitness coach, she currently hosts an array of virtual class offerings and detox packages to promote affordable, easy-to-access workouts and wellness tools. She also created Tabernacle, an artistic and movement based approach to healing and and self - care designed for to empower collective/community healing.

Additionally, she is the creator of AfroDGak – a confidence-centered program focusing sexual health education and consciousness intended to celebrate the black erotic by reimagining our sexual liberation and body autonomy.

In her current community organizer role at the ACLU of Oklahoma, she has focused on encouraging intersectional approaches to challenging systems of oppression in marginalized communities with a particular focus on racial justice, healing justice, and criminal justice reform. Utilizing artistic empowerment, she is also the co-founder of OKC Artists for Justice- a grassroots organization founded to provide advocacy for sexual assault survivors in the Daniel Holtzclaw case. She has been interviewed on national media outlets such as TV One, For Harriet, and the African American Policy Forum in addition to serving as a panelist at the 2016 Women of Color Expo and Columbia Law Intersectionality forum in NYC.

She was recognized for the 2017 Social Justice Activator Award from the YWCA of Oklahoma and the 2017 ACLU Angie Debo Civil Libertarian award for her many contributions in the state of Oklahoma. She was awarded the 2016 Community Impact Award presented by Perry Publishing and Broadcasting and the 2016 Woman of Action Award from the National Organization for Women.

Candace Liger is a queer, 30 something mother of 2, originally from Greenville, MS.

Julie Shapiro

Bachelors Degree of Arts in Psychology,
Bachelors Degree of Science in Hospitality,
Food Management and Science Studies.

IT WASN'T REALLY A WEIGHT PROBLEM
by Julie Shapiro

Blowing out the candles on my thirteenth birthday I had one wish. It was something I asked God to take away every night before I went to bed. Holding back tears in front of a room full of family, I closed my eyes tight, pretending to wish for something grand in the eyes of my family and blew out the candles. For me though nothing could be grander than being normal again. Being happy again and not worrying anymore. When I opened my eyes I thought for sure this wish would be granted and things would be the way they used to be!

The next morning, I woke up and the same daunting worries were on my mind. Nothing had changed. My brain was still infested with horrible thoughts. The same thoughts that clouded my mind since that fateful August afternoon.

> THE IRONY OF THIS WHOLE STORY IS THAT BEFORE ALL OF THIS STARTED, I NEVER HAD A PROBLEM WITH WEIGHT. I NEVER HAD AN ISSUE WITH BODY IMAGE, AND I NEVER WOULD HAVE THOUGHT THIS WAS EVER SOMETHING I WOULD HAVE TO WORRY ABOUT.

I was happy, healthy and active. I had a great childhood with loving parents, supportive sisters, and at the time could not have asked for things to have been better. As a child, I was always on the tentative side and usually always the last to learn something, but I never shied away from the experience; I always eventually learned or tried things. There was nothing in my childhood that I can remember that would have made my parents or myself believe that confidence, self image or self doubt would ever play a role in hindering my development, much less concern them with me having an issue with body image. Then on a warm sunny August day while basking in the last few weeks of summer vacation, everything changed. Pandora's box opened and my mind was flooded with unstoppable thoughts. I went from happy go lucky and carefree to quiet, cautious, and filled with fear.

It was the last week of summer camp and the annual trip to the water park was always the highlight of the whole summer. We waited months for this. This was why we went to camp. We thought we were so grown up. At the age of twelve, to go to the water park without our parents made us feel very independent and confident. The counselors were cool; they pretty much gave us the freedom to do as we pleased as long as we were back at the bus on time. It was the perfect summer day, warm, sunny and just right for a day at the park. When the bus pulled into the parking lot, we could hardly contain ourselves with excitement. We took our seats feverishly planning our day with friends. Once at the park we jumped out of our seats and as we exited the bus the counselors shouted "be back at 3:30pm" we barely heard them we were so ecstatic. Straight to the water park was our initial destination. We did not want to waste one minute of our time dawdling around. We knew it would get crowded fast and we didn't want to be held up in lines. Off we went basking in the sunshine, zipping down the water slides, having a great time. After endless runs on down the water slides my friends and I gathered to decide if it was time for lunch. We decided a few more runs would be better and then we could eat quickly and check out the rest of the park rides. On my way up to the top I felt something funny on the bottom of my foot. Thinking nothing of it, I picked up my foot and saw it was a band aid. "Gross", I thought, but with my mind on the ride, I quickly brushed it off and kept going. I made a quick mental note to wash my hands before I ate and forgot all about it. About an hour later, we decided enough was enough and it was time to eat lunch. We grabbed our lunches and sat at the table planning what we would do for the rest of the time. Finishing our lunches and our plan set, we cleaned up and headed out of the water park. As we were packing up, it hit me like a ton of bricks on the head; I had not gone and washed my hands. I just ate lunch with my hands, the hands that had touched that band-aid. What if a person who had HIV had worn that band-aid? Having just learned about this horrible disease in health class I became nervous. Could I have contracted HIV from that band-aid? Could I get sick? It was at that moment that a switch had been flipped in my brain the "on" button had been pushed and like a floodgate, the thoughts took over my mind and like flooding water rushing down a street they were unstoppable. I became terrified; it was at that moment my life changed forever.

My days became consumed with research, reading encyclopedias, searching the internet, and asking vague questions to counselors at camp. I prayed nightly that the tormenting thoughts of getting HIV would just stop. I became quiet, reserved. I became cautious, careful. I didn't want to get sick, I didn't want to do anything to set off my "compromised" immune system. I thought for sure once school started, that the thoughts would disappear, that I would be too consumed with homework, theater practice, etc, that I would not have time to think about it. It didn't. The light hearted things that most pre-teen, teenage kids thought about, talked about, and worried about, were not things that I thought about. I spent my time, reliving that specific moment at the water park when I made the decision to touch that band-aid. It became difficult to concentrate; I lost interest, what was the point? I was doomed to spend the rest of my days in a hospital bed, or so I thought. While my friends started going to parties, and talking about boys, I waited anxiously for symptoms that might begin popping up. Instead of counting days to homecoming, I was counting how many days it had been since I had touched that band-aid. As the days progressed, my behavior started changing too. All of a sudden the finger I had used brushing the band-aid off, I would not use it. When I saw a band-aid on a waitress at a restaurant I would not eat. I was constantly washing my hands every time I touched something that I believed was contaminated. I would not shake people's hands at church. Now not only was I obsessive in my thought patterns but also to calm those thoughts I started acting strangely and my parents started to Notice. My mom was the one who confronted me and asked me what was going on. When I told her she laughed it off. Told me not to be ridiculous and not to worry. She tried to talk me out of the nervousness and fear that I truly believed that I had HIV. She tried so hard to make me believe that it was not possible to contract HIV from a band-aid. She tried to explain that the chlorine in the water would have killed it. That HIV does not live outside of the body for very long. She made me watch the Greg Louganis story so that I could see that the doctor that helped him who was bare handed touched Greg's blood and did not get HIV to prove how difficult it was to get that way. She started stating facts about how it is contracted and even set up an appointment for me to talk to my pediatrician. It didn't matter though, my mind was convinced and nothing was louder than my mind. It hollered so loud, no amount of reason from my doctor was changing my mind. I wanted him to test me for it, but he said "No." He felt that I needed to overcome the issue without feeding into the fear. Getting tested would feed the fear and he was confident 100% that I was fine and I needed to see a psychiatrist. Angry and frustrated I left refusing to get help.

As the urges to wash my hands, purge of contaminated clothing got stronger and stronger, my behaviors became harder and harder to control and in turn, they became very obvious and frustrating to my parents, friends, and family. Every time I washed my hands my mom asked me why? Every time I needed to throw something out I got asked why? I found myself making up excuses, lying and feeling guilty. I needed to find something less conspicuous than my go to behaviors, that's when I found food. It was the one thing that I could turn to that was not going to be obvious and it calmed my mind just as well as washing my hands. If I could not control my thoughts then I would control my actions by eating. The calmness that overcame me with each bite was almost addicting. It felt good to be able to hide my feelings and not get questioned. It was easier to convince my parents that I was better. By the time I was a senior in high school I had gained 50 pounds. I was self-conscious, I was lacking self-esteem, and my body image was in the toilet. I could no longer shop in the stores I used to shop, because I had gone from a junior 6-8 to a women's 12-14 and I was heading towards 16's. Shorts, tank tops and a bathing suit were out of the question. I was disgusted, but I thought it was the only option I had. With this plummeting self confidence came declining friendships. It was not long before I was besties with "Ben and Jerry's." Ben and Jerry didn't care that I was gaining weight, they didn't question me, and they were simply there to quell my thoughts. To feel a little more like I had a social life or at least feel like I was a normal teenager, I spent my afternoons living vicariously through reruns of 90210.

Before I knew it, I was graduating high school and going off to college; It was my chance, I thought, to start fresh. One of the perks of going to college was getting a physical and getting up to date with blood work and vaccinations. Knowing that my new doctor could not go to my parents because I was eighteen, thank you HIPPA, I was able to get blood work done. I was given a new lease on life. I was given a clean bill of health from my doctor. Finally knowing for sure that the band-aid at the park had not given me HIV, was surely just what I needed to get these obsessive thoughts out of my head; or so

I thought. The scale at the doctor's office left me less than thrilled at the self-sabotaging. I spent that summer in pants and short sleeve shirts to cover my thighs and arms. I tried to prepare for preseason- as I was going into college as a varsity athlete, but it was so hard. The runs were unbearable on my knees and my runs consisted of me telling myself to "just finish fatso."

" You are a disgusting disgrace."

" I can't believe you let yourself get this way."

" How could you do this to yourself?"

" What a jerk you are."

 The self-loathing was incredible. The amount of self-hate that I generated that summer was extremely intense and even though I was not binging my way through the summer, the weight seemed to not budge. I tried my best to keep up with the workouts but my best, to me, was never good enough.

Despite the discouraging summer, I was excited to go to college. I was playing tennis on the varsity team, I was making friends and things were starting to look up. I hit the tennis courts and worked hard during the season with the results of dropping 20 pounds because I was not compulsively eating to calm my mind; plus dining hall food was less than desirable. It felt good, I was gaining confidence; I thought I had for sure kicked this thing to the curb. I had finally beaten it.

Then like a slap in the face the obsessive thoughts started bombarding my mind again. This time, it was not that I had HIV, but that I could get HIV from contaminated things from my tennis team. During a team trip one of the girls got a blister from her sneakers and her heel was bleeding. She grabbed some bandages, and antiseptic. Cleaned it up threw her sneakers and blood stained socks in her bag. She then threw her bag in the van on top of all the other bags. I froze, what if it was on my bag, what if it leaked through her bag and stained my bag. I was silently freaking out. The whole ride home I was quiet on the outside, but on the inside my brain was screaming. I started crying, I could not help it, It was uncontrollable. My teammates were concerned. They could not understand why I was upset, I had won my match, and I played well. I was smiling and having fun not a few hours earlier. I made up an excuse that I thought I had eaten something bad and that my stomach was in a lot of pain; they bought it, but not for long. With the resurgence of the obsessive thoughts came the compulsions.

The urge to wash, toss, and avoid, was ten times stronger than it was the first time around. I was throwing out contaminated clothes like it was my job. I was washing my hands until they were red, and my self-confidence and fun loving personality disappeared as quickly as it had come back. My teammates started to notice. They started to question. I had to do something, but there was no way I was going to gain all that weight back. I felt good. I looked good, and people noticed the weight loss. It was exhilarating and it was empowering. There had to be another way to quell the thoughts. Again I turned to food. But rather than over consuming food, I began to restrict it. The less I ate, the more I lost. The more I lost the more I was complimented, it was powerful and it was perfect. It was a perfect way to hide my true problem.

I came home from college another 20lbs lighter. Everyone noticed. It was awesome. It gave me something else to focus on. I joined a gym that summer and started taking fitness classes. I loved the feeling I got from working out. My obsessions shifted from worrying about getting sick to getting fat. I was so afraid I would revert to old ways that I hit the gym hard core. I gave myself reasons to not eat. I took a part time job, went to summer school and spent my time at the gym. I ran myself ragged and was eating toast and milk for breakfast, sweet potatoes for lunch and a piece of grilled chicken for dinner. If I veered from this regiment I panicked. Being preoccupied with studying, work, and gym helped me to maintain my schedule. As the summer progressed, and the self-sustained stress mounted my body

beYOUtiful

started to revolt.

I had the shakes, my hair was falling out and my skin was getting dry. I attributed the shakes to drinking too much coffee, my hair while it was scary, I attributed to stress at school. The dry skin I really didn't think too much about it was summer after all and much of my time was spent in the air conditioning. Then one night I woke up, I had a funny pain in my stomach, I went to the bathroom thinking that might help. It didn't. I thought maybe I'm just hungry; I will grab something small and go back to bed. I had to be up early anyways so I would consider that breakfast and head out to work. I never went into work that day. The pain spread, down my shoulder, into my back, across my stomach, before I could even think, I was doubled over screaming in pain. My dad came running out and rushed me to the hospital.

> THE WHOLE RIDE I WAS THRIVING IN UNBELIEVABLE PAIN.

We barely made it in the ER I was screaming and crying and crying and apologizing. The woman who was registering us called a nurse and I was whisked into the ER.

On my way to get an ultrasound, the nurse was asking me routine questions about my height and weight. After I gave her my weight I asked her if the weight and height were normal. If she thought I was fat. She stared at me and said, "I wish I could be your height and weight." "You are perfect for your height." She rolled me into the room and the tech came in. The nurse told me she would be back to get me in a bit. She brought me back to my room and my parents were there waiting for me. All of a sudden, I had to use the bathroom. I was barefoot and the bathroom was about 100 feet away and I was hooked to an IV. I asked my mom for my shoes and she told me she had put them in the car. I freaked out. I lost it. There was no way on this God given earth I was walking barefoot to the bathroom on a dirty hospital floor. What if I stepped on a syringe? What if I stepped in blood? I was furious. My mom understood exactly what was going on; it had nothing to do with not having my shoes, it had everything to do with me not getting over my fear of diseases. That the strict regiment I was putting myself on was to control my intrusive thoughts, the food restriction, the over emphasis on homework, the added stress I was putting on myself to take extra shifts at work; They were all to minimize my need to worry. That day I was given an ultimatum. I was either going to get help from a psychiatrist or I was not going back to school in August. With only 4 weeks left, I wanted to go back. I had friends, I loved my classes, I enjoyed playing tennis and all of it was going to be taken from me if I did not agree to get help. I agreed with a condition. That I get that help back at school. I promised that when I got back to school I would go to the health center and get a referral.

Knowing my mom would pull me from school in a heartbeat, when I got to school for preseason my sophomore year, I went straight to the health center. It happened to be perfect timing. The college was starting a new program with local mental health professionals to come onto campus and be a resource to students that needed it. If we needed more that a few sessions then we could get it covered under our health insurance. Knowing I would need more than one or two I called my mom and had her get things situated with the college and my insurance to get my help. I was diagnosed with Obsessive Compulsive Disorder and Disordered Eating. It was with this psychologist that I was introduced to meditation. Along with my primary care physician getting me on some anti anxiety meds, the psychologist had me doing daily meditation. We set up a gym schedule with boundaries that helped me to learn the difference between healthy exercise and using it to reduce anxiety rather than abusing it and using it as a crutch. I learned to understand that I had control over my situations and that I needed to develop language that was going to help me deal with my anxiety. I came to understand that my OCD was fueling my Disordered Eating and that while these things are part of me but it did not define me. I learned to have a healthy relationship with food. With this healthy new outlook on food, exercise and life, I became intrigued with teaching group exercise classes. I wanted to know more and spent time studying to become a certified group exercise instructor. I worked hard not only

be YOUtiful

to maintain a healthy weight but to also have a healthy relationship with food and myself. Having worked hard to get my group exercise certification, I was given an opportunity for on campus job of teaching classes. I was stoked. I began making more friends, I was having fun and it felt good. My self-esteem was beginning to rise. My senior year of college came quicker than I had ever imagined. I was playing tennis, I was having fun with friends, and I had learned to love myself and have some self-respect and confidence. I was still working weekly with the psychologist and I felt myself getting better feeling more like the fun loving "kid" now young adult, I had planned on becoming. As senior year progressed I was still teaching exercise classes, but my regular classes were getting intense. I was still practicing my meditation nightly, but I was still feeling anxious. These were things that I was working with the doctor with but I still felt like something was missing. I was flipping through the channels on TV and found Ashtanga Yoga. I fell in love. It was an amazing combination of the feel good fitness benefits, along with the meditation practices that I maintained as I worked with the psychologist. I made it part of my morning routine. I woke up a bit earlier, did yoga, got ready and headed out to class. At night before bed, I listened to my meditation CD's. It helped. It was exactly what I needed to round out my self-care practice. Interestingly, the last semester of my senior year I took the psychology of Buddhist meditation. It was as if the college had dropped that class in my lap as a congratulations for working so hard on your studies and yourself. BAM mind blown.

> WHEN I FINISHED THE CLASS I KNEW I HAD TO TEACH YOGA AND I KNEW THAT I HAD TO SHARE MY EXPERIENCE WITH OTHERS.

After graduation I spent the summer teaching group exercise classes, getting certified as a personal trainer and I took my first job at a local YMCA. I then started going to yoga classes and reconnected with my love of yoga. I decided that it was integral to my personal growth to understand why yoga was such a powerful force in helping me heal. I became certified as a 200hr yoga teacher. Looking back on the experience, I thought it was a weight problem, but it wasn't.

www.beyoutifulbooks.com

The reality was I needed to come to terms with and get a handle on my own fears. I was using food in both ways, overconsumption and under consumption to fuel the fire rather than put it out. Since then, through teaching yoga and fitness classes I have been using my experience to empower women to take charge of their life and be accountable for their understanding why, they truly turn to food when they are struggling with their weight. I encourage women to look at themselves and question why they are choosing to eat what they eat. I have learned that we have a choice and what we choose to do is what leads us down the path that we follow. I also learned that even though we might make the wrong choice the right choice is never far away and we can always choose to change our direction. The power and the choice is ours and ours alone. For so long, I spent so much time resenting myself for having that time in my life. I spent so much time I wishing I could have gone back in time and changed that fateful day. I daydreamed about how I would have told myself to go and wash my hands. I should have scrapped the band-aid off with the step rather than touching it. I spent so much time replaying that day that I forgot how to appreciate what I had at that moment. It has taken a great deal of time to forgive myself for the resentment. However, part of my ability to be successful as a fitness professional was taking that time to forgive myself and to use my story to fuel motivation and inspiration to other women.

It has been 21 years since that day at the water park. I cannot really believe that much time has passed. The lessons I learned from that fateful day have made me who I am today. I don't regret that day anymore. I appreciate the experience. I feel that it has made me more compassionate and empathetic to the needs of my clients and the growth of my business. Today I have an amazing career as a fitness professional and most importantly I have a healthy relationship with food. I have a positive self-image, and I am confident in my abilities to be the best l can be. Are there days that those fears pop up, yes, but I can handle them so much better than ever before. I attribute my ability to snuff out the fear because I have learned to forgive myself, to be patient with myself. I remind myself daily that food does not have the answer to my problems. I have the answer to my problems with in me. For me it was a weight problem, but it wasn't. I used food to hide and as a result my weight suffered. It suffered greatly.

Now that I understand this I am able to move forward and create the life that I want and I will not be hindered or deterred from being happy, healthy and self confident.

Biography of Julie Shapiro

Julie has been in the fitness industry for 10 years in a variety of roles. She has been a weight loss consultant for a major weight loss company, certified personal trainer, yoga teacher and group exercise instructor. Julie has a Bachelors Degree of Arts in Psychology and a Bachelors Degree of Science in Hospitality, Food Management and Science Studies. She has worked with a variety of women to help them achieve their goals in a healthy and non aggressive manner. Helping women and girls see fitness as a means to be healthy and set goals that are attainable are some of the things that Julie works on with her clients. Her goal is to help her clients reach their goals!

Dee Dee Grayson

BS. Ed., CLC, CBE, CCMF, PCD (DONA)

BEHIND THE MASK
By Dee Dee Grayson

Hair, makeup, nails, clothes, purses and shoes. These were the love of my life. I was so cute! I loved to look good and I felt good, too. I did not realize that looking good was so important to me until my husband pointed it out. I had lost even the basics. As a child of the 60's we were taught to always look your best leaving the house. What had happened? Why didn't I care any more? Where was the diva in me?

It is the year 1993 and I am exhausted yet triumphant after giving birth to my fourth child, a beautiful and healthy baby girl! Oh, but this was no ordinary birth. No, not so! For this child was my first that I delivered vaginally! Hallelujah! Praises be unto the God of all creation! You see, I had a talk with the Lord some months back and I was determined not to have the experience that I had with my last delivery.

Wait a minute!

Hold the phone!

I am getting a little ahead of myself. Allow me to digress and go back to the beginning where all this got started…

> I AM STROLLING THROUGH CAMPUS AND WHAT DO MY EYES SEE BUT A REAL FINE BROTHER WHO IS ON THE BASKETBALL TEAM.
> "OH, HE MAKES MY TASTE BUDS WATER!"

Oh yeah, that's right look this way and behold. Now you may not readily see the athletic prowess of this sister. My 5' 8" frame, weighing in at just under 125 pounds soaking wet, belittled its achievements: Female Athlete of the Year in high school, 1980 Big East All State, and starting guard for the Murray State Aggietts making their first appearance in the NJCAA Tournament where we placed 5th in the country. Yes, this sister had it going on and this good-looking man did take notice. Well, one thing led to another and I eventually found myself explaining to my parents that I was pregnant. Wow! Now that was an experience!

My family was a God-fearing strain of folk; you know the type that had very strict and conservative rules compared to most other families. As the second child of eight siblings, I was determined not to let that background slow me down toward reaching my goals. In high school, I desperately wanted to play basketball. But my father and mother laid down the law on how I was going to be able to do that. In no uncertain terms they stated that I must be on the high school's honor roll in order to fulfill that desire. Since they deemed it necessary for me to do it, I did so. Upon bringing home my accomplishment, they were obliged to let me play; and play I did. Okay, back to the problem at hand.

I was in college and I was pregnant. My family took that news pretty hard. I, myself, felt somewhat overwhelmed. But I knew what had to be done, so I fixed my heart and mind on the task at hand – having this child. It was a relatively normal pregnancy. I did not have anything unusual happen until my last trimester. I felt my water break, but because I had no understanding of what that meant, so I wandered around for a couple of days thereafter. It was when my back started hurting that I decided to make another appointment with my OBGYN.

The first visit was a real shocker! I had to be examined! I had to be inspected! I had to be probed! Oh, how humiliating was that position on the table – spread-eagled before all of God's creation! Glad that was over. So this visit was less intrusive. At least physically, anyway. The doctor explained to me that this was an emergency situation. My water had broken and emptied the uterus of the life giving, life protecting amniotic fluid within. My precious child was now a liability to me. His new state compromised my life because there was no protection for us from which that fluid had so marvelously provided. Although it was early, my baby had to come out. I expressed to the doctor that I wanted every effort to be given to allow my son to live – even if it meant that my own health would be further compromised. He further stated that there were no beds available in the nearest facilities in Oklahoma City, the nearest hospital that could best accommodate my baby and I. I had to be transported via helicopter to an appropriate hospital in Tulsa. My mom decided that she would accompany me on the flight. She and I did not have much to say, though. I know that I was churning like a whirlwind had lifted me up and carried me aloft. But my athletic training allowed me to continue to focus on the task at hand: I am going to be a first time mom. I am going to have a newborn. He will be born some 10 weeks early. He will need special care.

Upon arriving at St. Francis Hospital, I was admitted and to my surprise and utter amazement I had to wait as the medical team tended to a patient who was said to need more immediate attention. I thought that if this was the case, she must be near death since I had to be life-flighted to here from Seminole. I continued to lie on the table while waiting for the emergency operating procedures to save my life and that of my unborn child. The surgery was successful and I was able to survive along with my precious baby boy. The doctor mumbled something to me as I was coming around from the effects of the anesthesia that my mother later explained. He basically said that I would probably have had trouble carrying a child to full term anyway due to the narrowness of my pelvis. Of course that was just noise to me at the time, I had a new priority; I had a son to tend to. I was somewhat dismayed that I could not touch or hold him very long; he was so tiny, I could hold him in one hand. He had so many tubes in him when I later viewed him. The doctor said that he had to let him cry for 24 hours and if that went well then he would be okay. The Lord was merciful and my son left the hospital after 30 days of being in the neonatal ICU. He was home for Christmas. Now that was my first-born; but the journey has just begun.

Now let's fast-forward about six years later. I met the love of my life who loves me as I need to be loved. We go on to marry and eight years after my first child I was now expecting another. Well, due to the fact that I couldn't exactly pinpoint when my pregnancy began, my OBGYN decided to subject me to an amniocentesis to better determine the age of my pregnancy.

Did I tell you how much I appreciated being on the OBGYN's table? That appreciation was lowered much further after that painful experience.

He believed that his estimate was about right and we proceeded on schedule. I had requested to have a natural childbirth. In my mind, there had been eight years since I had had the previous C-section and whatever problems or difficulties that were present then, I believed that the marvelous way that the Creator had put my body together had allowed it to heal; the doctor disagreed. In his understanding, I was a high-risk patient because of the nature of my previous experience and the comments that the surgeon left in my medical file. He assured me that we would take every precaution and try to fulfill my desire. At least that was what I was led to believe. Since I had no other cause to doubt him, I acknowledged his concern and we proceeded on with the birth of my second child. My husband was so excited as he paced along the wall of the room awaiting the child's birth. I remember looking at the monitor and laboring for a few hours before the nurse came and told me that she could give me something for pain. I graciously declined; however, after they repeated this several times, I was somewhat eager to receive that medication to ease some of the pain.

To my astonishment I found myself awakening as I was being wheeled to an operating room. The doctor had consulted with my husband after my "pain" medication was administered. He convinced my husband that since I had labored all night long and had not been able to come to the needed 10cm dilation for the natural birth of my child that surgery was necessary. My husband would also tell me later that during my labor just before the administering of that "pain" medication, one of the nurses informed him that I had dilated to an 8. I was only 2cm away from feeling like I was a real woman! All of my past accomplishments began slipping into the distant background. I now felt like a failure, a failure at the task that the Creator had made me to do; I could not give birth to a child like He had ultimately designed. I resigned myself to the surgery and we had a healthy baby girl. She was adorable. Well, as much as I could enjoy her anyway. My loving husband had become so enamored with her that I nor anyone else could have any quality time with the child. Cute. I was able to come home with my baby. Aside from a little nausea, I was fine too. At least for the time being.

Some two years later, my husband was eager to try for another child. I was not so eager. But I was gently persuaded into agreement. And so I became pregnant with my third child. My mind now races back to the humiliating experience with my first daughter. Maybe this will be different. My husband now has a good job and we have decent insurance. Maybe, just maybe, things will be better this go-around. I find myself exhaling a long breath after my new OBGYN repeats to me the same mumbo-jumbo that I heard from my previous doctor. Namely, that I was a high-risk patient because of my first pregnancy and now, in addition, to that fact I just had another C-section a little over two years ago. Even though in my own mind that was plenty of time for the Father in heaven to cause my body to heal, I again acquiesce to his professional understanding of the situation. After all he is an OBGYN, a professional in his field.

It turns out that just before the date set for the operation I went into labor. Upon getting to the hospital, I believed that everything was going to be okay. That early labor should have been a sign that things were not going to go as smoothly this time around. I am informed that my doctor is still at the clinic and I am to proceed with the surgery preparation. A nurse comes into the room to give me some medication just before the anesthesiologist. Once the medication is given, I state to her that I am feeling rather strange. I feel like something starting at the top of my head is slowing coming down my face. The nurse exclaims that it is my blood pressure dropping and then quickly administers another medication to counteract the effects. My husband is looking at me rather astonished and I am now thinking, "Lord please don't let these people kill me!" She leaves and, as expected, the anesthesiologist comes in to give me the epidural. He explains to me why it is necessary and the effects of the medication. He then calmly proceeds to do his job of finding a proper spot in betwixt my vertebrae in the spinal column to insert his long needle. He asks me to bend over more as I am sitting on the edge of the bed. No sooner than he sticks the needle in my back, my right leg promptly extends without my command and knocks over the bedside table in front of me. Surprised, and somewhat annoyed over this situation, the doctor continues to find another spot as he states that I am very bony and it is difficult to find a good location. My fear is mounting at the prospect of being seriously harmed. My husband is now on edge, too. Once the doctor finishes and exits, I whisper to my husband, "Don't let them kill me."

Soon we are in the operating room to experience a lighter side of this journey. The OBGYN is busy cleaning up some scar tissue as my husband stands near my head and the anesthesiologist is over my head. We can whiff the ranking foul smell of burnt flesh and almost cringe in disgust when the anesthesiologist retorts in his Indonesian accent, "We no bar-B-Q you." We all chuckle. This is not at all amusing to the OBGYN who is carefully performing his craft. He snorts, "Don't make her laugh!" We all become quiet. My honey then moves a little further towards the action of the birth to watch how they perform the C-section.

> HE IS AMAZED TO SEE THE DOCTOR PULLING VIGOROUSLY AS HE ATTEMPTS TO FREE MY THIRD CHILD FROM THE UTERUS. ONCE FREED, I FEEL MY VEINS GET WARM AGAIN AND I BECOME VERY GROGGY AND SOMEWHAT INCOHERENT JUST AFTER THEY INTRODUCE ME TO MY NEW BABY GIRL.

A short time later, I hear my honey describing the birthing process to me but I am too woozy to understand. He tells me later when I am taken to my room where I am resting with him by my bedside. I ask him to call for the nurse. I believe that I am trying to maintain a sense of calm for his sake as I am feeling rather nauseated.

When she comes in I am told that I went to the bathroom and began to regurgitate strongly; Honey is a little concerned about me. Later the nurse brings my new daughter into the room and lays her on my chest. I am oblivious to her presence. She is taken back to the nursery and cared for there. My honey is now disturbed over my condition. He begins to wonder what have they done to me to cause me to have so much trouble. Again my daughter is brought to the room a day or so later and I attempt to hold her. I have to call for the nurse again. This time it is only dry heaving. This happens another day before the vomiting and dry-heaving cycle subsides and I am released from the hospital with my healthy baby girl. I am still very weak and still somewhat incoherent. My days at this point all seem a blur. Honey tells his supervisor at his job that he will not return until he is comfortable with how I am healing. He knows that he has about 12 weeks that he can spend. He will take all of it for the first and only time.

It was during this time that I had the battle of my life. The battle for my sanity as well as my newborn's safety. After I started returning to normalcy from all the drugs given to me in the hospital, I started sinking into another world I did not want to go into. This was a dark and very cold-like world. Devoid of real feeling. Out of touch with self and surroundings. My gracious honey had been so helpful by taking off so much time from work and helping me adjust. But now it was just my daughters and me. All I wanted to do was sleep. "Leave me alone and don't bother me." "I have a newborn and a three year old at home and I need to be a mother." "How can I be a mother and I don't think I'm a good mother!" "I'm a failure!" "My birth experience was stolen from me!" "How can I take care of anyone!" "Nobody listened to me!" "No one acknowledged me! Leave me alone, leave me alone, leave me alone!" These thoughts and others filled my tormented mind.

But I was wearing my mask very well. My husband did recognize that something was wrong and he would ask me, "Honey are you alright?" "Honey how are you?" My masked response was "I'm doing wonderful!" "I'm good!" However, that was so far from the truth. The truth is I was a mental mess! My thoughts were everywhere, I feigned doing well by getting up out of bed and getting dressed pretending that my health was awesome! How could I tell my husband that I needed professional help because of my mental health? He had already dealt with mental illness in his family. How could I take him through that again?

So my mask was really cemented to my face. I would not tell anyone what was going through my head! Who would I ask for help, where would I go? If I were tell they would take my baby away from me. If I told they would give me a pill. I didn't want people to think that I was crazy. Mental health problems in the black community were practically a taboo subject, especially at this time; you just did not talk about such things. I did not understand at the time that my hormones were out of whack. My doctor, let alone any nurse, said nothing to me about the hormonal changes that I would experience. My own care diminished during this time as well. I was angry! Angry all the time and I ate to compensate for my feelings. I gained much weight and I desired not to dress up. Going to church was a chore for that very reason. I just skipped the makeup, grabbed a decent looking skirt and went on.

My thoughts took a turn for the worse. I began to have thoughts of harming the beautiful little girl in my arms. They became so prevalent that I put a pillow over her face and only by the grace of the Lord my God did I remove that pillow and walk out the room.
After this incident, I still did not seek help or try to remove my mask. As the Lord graciously brought me through this dark hour in my life, I found myself pregnant once again.

Remember I told you earlier that I had a talk with the Lord? Well, this is when I had that talk. You see, being in that room with that nurse giving me that medication and realizing that these people could kill me with the epidural process, I was determined then not to allow that to ever – yes, I mean ever happen again. Did you hear me? Let me say it again – I mean never to let that happen again.

Now I was going to have to travel down that road. I am pregnant again and I know what my doctor is going to tell me. No one will tell me what I am able to do. If I die, it will be by my own accord. If I did die then I believed that I would be in the kingdom of heaven. Let's do this! The battle is on!

I talked with my physician and just as predictable as flies to spoiled food, he told me the direction he wanted me to go and that it was best to have another C-section. I contended somewhat with him concerning the idea but resolved in my heart and mind that he could say what he wanted. He could even do what he thought best. I could show him better that I could tell him. Dee Dee was going to take back her birthing process; this time around was going to be different. I would make sure of it. The doctor gave me the scheduled date of the surgery expecting all to proceed as planned. I patiently waited for my fourth child to tell me when it was time to be born. When the morning of the date of the surgery came, the nurse called me. She asked if I remembered that I was to have surgery today. I firmly told her that I was not having surgery and that I was still resting. I reminded her that I had expressed this before and then promptly hung up the phone. I felt a sigh of relief. I had taken the first step. I had made them aware of my personal intentions and it was not according to their plans.

A few weeks later I felt the first signs that my baby was ready to come into the world. My honey drove me to the clinic near the hospital. A physician whom I had not seen before came in and began to consult with me. "I have heard about you. You are the one who did not show up for surgery. What is it that you want to do?"

I was happy.
I was elated.
They were listening.

I told him that it was my deepest desire to have this child vaginally. He explained to me that there were no formal studies or medical cases known about a patient with my particular background. I was unique. So he would permit me to go through with this process but if at any point in time, he felt a danger to the child, or me it would be back to the operating room. I tentatively acknowledged his counsel and proceeded to go next door to the hospital as instructed. There I delivered my baby vaginally without any complications. Hallelujah! Praises be to the name of the Lord!

That chapter of the story ended 23 years ago. The journey, on the other hand, continued. I went on to have three little boys vaginally! I really took back my birthing process; I am so happy that I did! I must confess that I am in recovery from my Postpartum PTSD. I realize that I was indeed traumatized from the births that were hijacked from me. A wonderful therapist is counseling me. She does not like for me to say that about her, but that is who she is to me. When I'm ready to talk she listens. I was so messed up that I did not want anything to do with births. My precious friend is a very wonderful Advanced Birth and Postpartum Doula. She listens to me. She watches me so intently as I sob in the midst of sentences. Today I can say that healing is taking place. She loves what she is doing and I wholeheartedly agree that she is fabulous! Before I began to process what had happened to me, just at the mention of something about birth I would become angry and upset. "Don't talk to me about birth, I don't want to hear it!" would be my response. Now, I am looking forward to my training to become a Birth Doula!

My body image definitely changed through my birthing journey. I went from a size 10/12 to a size 22. My diva card was burned up. Going through this journey definitely changed how I viewed myself. I have not begun to process that part, yet, but I will. I am happy to say that I am no longer a size 22 but a size 16.

I ask that you crack your mask and say, "Honey, I am not well, I need help. Let me tell you what is going on with me." There are resources that are available to help in dealing with Postpartum depression, Postpartum anxiety or OCD, Postpartum PTSD (post traumatic stress), Bipolar disorder or mania and Postpartum psychosis.

PSI Postpartum Support International
1-800-944-4733

Postpartum Progress
help@postpartumprogress.org

Suicide Prevention Hotline
1-800-273-8255

I am so happy to say that my mask is cracked and the pieces are falling off daily. Crack your mask by saying I need help!

The journey to healing will begin.

Biography of Dee Dee Grayson

Dee Dee is the very blessed mom of Jesse, Jerece, JaLeisa, Jade, Jerry II, Joshua and Josiah. Grandmother of Luke and the precious wife of Jerry Sr. She loves singing, reading, drawing, photography, scrapbooking and traveling!

Dee Dee began her birth work journey in 2014 by becoming a Certified Lactation Counselor. She has served as the COBA Baby Cafe Assistant Director and Facilitator in the minority program.

Dee Dee serves families through her business Bountiful Blessings Birth and Postpartum Doula Services. She supports and nurtures as the families prepare to meet their bundle(s) of joy.

Dee Dee's plans for the future include travel and obtaining her IBCLC credential.

Allyson Reneau

*A Business Woman,
Gymnastics Coach & Judge,
Mother to 11 Children.*

Chapter 6

HOUSEWIFE TO HARVARD:
GOD HAS AN EXTRAORDINARY PLAN FOR YOU!
By Allyson Reneau

Have you ever felt discouraged, stuck, hopeless, and unable to dream about doing more with your life? I know I did. I was forty-eight years old and a little past my prime; but inside of myself, I hoped I was destined to accomplish something significant. However, circumstances and difficulties kept me from even dreaming about it. I knew that I had much to be thankful for: I was a mother to eleven beautiful, healthy children (yes, I had them all with the same man!) great friends, and a business I enjoyed very much. But something was missing. I intended to pray—actually pester God--until I had some direction for a change.

It was a cold, crisp January morning in 2011. The newly fallen snow was crunching beneath my feet, and the first burst of sunrise was climbing over the horizon. I was finishing my morning run before the kids woke up and I started my daily routine. I muttered the same prayer beneath my frozen breath that I had spoken for nearly two years.

> "Is this all there is to my life?" As I had many days, weeks, and months before, I waited for a message—a sign—something to break me free to serve humanity on a worldwide scale. I rounded the final curve to head for home, and instantly I knew; I must go to Harvard University.

I tried for a moment to wrap my head around that. I was fifty years old. I had eleven children. Seven were still at home. Three were in college. I had seventy-six hours remaining to finish my bachelor's degree. I lived in Oklahoma City, almost 2000 miles away from Boston. I certainly didn't have any extra money! I shared my idea with my closest friends for feedback. Interestingly enough, every one of them said, "Go for it!" I knew I wasn't qualified and certainly was not smart enough.

Forbes magazine published research from a study conducted at Stanford University. Psychologist Dr. Carol Dweck has spent her entire career studying people's attitude and how it relates to their performance in life. She has determined that your attitude is a greater predictor of your success than your IQ. Isn't that awesome? She says there are two categories of attitude: a fixed mindset or a growth mindset. A fixed mindset is the belief that you are unable to change, and a growth mindset embraces challenges and sees them as an opportunity to learn and change.

People with a growth mindset see failures and setbacks as

information to better themselves—instead of labeling it as failure. They are problem solvers. In other words, your success in life is determined on how you deal with these failures and challenges. The good news is that no matter what category of attitude you fall into, you can develop a growth mindset. Thomas Edison, who invented the light bulb said, "I have not failed. I've just found 10,000 ways that won't work." He also said, "Many of life's failures are people who did not realize how close they were to success when they gave up."

Armed with this information, I decided to attend a reception for potential Master's students in June of 2011 and ask the hard questions. One of my friends donated frequent flyer miles, and another hotel reward points. I was on my way to Boston! I attended the event and met Sarah Powell, who ultimately became my academic advisor, and was with me every step of the way. When I asked if I could do my education online, she said "No! Of course not! You are going to commute from Oklahoma City to Boston every week." I couldn't believe what I was hearing; She actually believed I could do it.

I flew home and made a list of every organization I could ask for a scholarship. And I asked for it all—weekly airfare, hotel, books and tuition. And the first group I asked said, "Yes!" Now here I am a few years later, not just a housewife with a high school education, but I actually graduated from Harvard this past May 2016 with straight A's. An education at Harvard is extraordinary—and life altering—and has opened so many wonderful doors for me, including working at NASA Headquarters in Washington D. C. I am so glad I took this leap of faith—and so can you!

A nurse who took care of dying people took notes for many years of their life's regrets and put her findings in a book. I think you may be amazed by the #1 regret. I was sure it was going to say, "I did not spend enough time with family and friends." But instead the top regret was: "I did not have the courage to pursue the dreams in my heart because of other people's opinions." Many looked back and could see clearly their unfulfilled dreams. Most of the people had not even accomplished half of them. Health brings a freedom very few realize, until they no longer have it.

Just remember, with God--and just a little faith in yourself, you can make the impossible possible. I certainly was not the smartest person in the Harvard classrooms, but I will tell you that my persistent attitude made up for it. Pursue your passion, be relentless, and never give up. Take the bad breaks as God guiding you in another direction. Flow with Him and watch yourself accomplish dreams you never thought possible. End this life with no regrets!

"Then Caleb quieted the people before Moses, and said, "Let us go up at once and take possession of the land; for we will certainly conquer it."
Numbers 13:30

Biography of Allyson Reneau

Allyson Reneau is a business woman, gymnastics coach and judge, and is mother to 11 children.

After putting off a lifelong dream of finishing her education, she enrolled at the University of Oklahoma and completed 76 hours in just 3 semesters to finish her BA in Communications with a 4.0 GPA.....all while juggling 7 kids at home and running a highly competitive gymnastics program training Olympic hopefuls. Allyson has worked with hundreds of state, regional, and national gymnastics champions.

In Fall 2011, at the age of 50, she entered the Masters program at Harvard in the field of International Relations. She travels 4000 miles weekly between her base in Oklahoma City and Boston for her classes. She currently maintains a 4.0 and plans to finish her degree in the Fall of 2015.

In addition, Allyson auditioned at Juilliard (piano) in January of 2012 and has been attending for 3 semesters.

Allyson has been invited to the United Nations several times to meet with the Executive Director of Worldwide Humanitarian Projects and the Director of Protection for Women and Children.

She has a dream to help as many women and girls as possible to find their purpose in life through education and entrepreneurship.

Also, she has just completed a joint research project between Harvard and the Naval War College on "Mentoring in the Military." This article was recently published in two journals.

To give substance to her emerging interest in space activities, Allyson was a participant in the 2014 Space Studies Program of the International Space University in Montreal, Canada, and returned as a Teaching Assistant for the 2015 program held at Ohio University in Athens, Ohio.

Allyson has been featured on FOX News, NBC, ABC, the Today Show, and in countless magazines and newspapers around the world.

Jennifer Armstrong

*Certified Nutrition &
Wellness Consultant*

HEALING AND RESTORATION:
HOW A JOURNEY TO HEAL MYSELF LED ME TO HELP OTHERS
By Jennifer Armstrong

Honestly I have never really had an issue with my weight until after I had children. As a child I had a very healthy appetite and absolutely loved food. My family always laughed and joked about how I was always the first kid to the table and would make sure there was nothing left on my plate. I loved hanging out in the kitchen with my Grandma because I knew I could be the taste tester. Despite my love for food, I never struggled with my weight. I remember being called

Olive Oil after having my tonsil removed because I didn't eat for about a week and when I returned to school, my socks would not stay up around my ankles. My mother and I did not have a car for many years and we relied on the city bus to get us anywhere we needed to go. This required a lot of walking, to and from the bus stops and maybe even further if I missed my bus. I ran track my sophomore year of high school and that was the first time I learned how to build muscle and really workout hard.

By the time I got to college I had gained some weight, but it was nothing to really worry about. I was kind of prepared to gain a little weight since everyone I knew warned me about the dreaded "freshman fifteen". I had my first child in 2005 and was surprised that within weeks of his arrival I could wear all my pre-pregnancy clothes. For the next couple of years my weight went up and down, but I was so focused on being a mother and working that I didn't really have time to notice or even care. I remember my Aunt telling me jokingly, "It's a thin line between fat and fine". I guess it was her way of telling me I was putting on a little weight.

In 2008 I had a traumatic miscarriage in the fifth month of my pregnancy, which left me depressed and devastated. I literally had days where I stayed in bed and cried all day. During this time I had a major falling out with my mother, who wasn't supportive in my time of grief. Feeling lost and hurt, I pushed forward somehow with the love and support of my husband and family. My doctor was ready to prescribe anti-depressants, but my husband said, "No!" He told me that it was natural for me to experience the sadness and pain I was in and that I could take as much time as I needed to heal myself. His love and understanding for me was amazing. We went to Mexico for vacation and I was finally able to breathe.

Shortly after we returned home, I found out that not only was I pregnant again, I was carrying twins. I was in complete shock to say the least. The doctor told me to be careful and take it easy. Then one day it happened again. I was at work when I felt cramps and began spotting. I immediately called my doctor and went into the office. I was terrified to hear that I lost another baby. One of the twins that I was carrying had miscarried. It's a condition called Vanishing Twin Syndrome in which one of a set of twin/multiple fetuses disappears in the uterus. In my case my body started to try to eliminate to deceased fetus, putting the remaining twin at risk of being miscarried. My doctor put me on complete bed rest for the remainder of my pregnancy and I had to go through a major procedure called a cervical cerclage to stitch my cervix closed in an attempt to keep the fetus.

I was seeing a specialist every two weeks because my pregnancy was considered high risk due to all of my complications. On March 11th I gave birth to a beautiful, healthy baby girl. Following the birth of my daughter, my father in law went into liver failure and was in and out of the hospital for months. It was really touch and go for him and caused a great deal of stress and uncertainty for our entire family. My father in law pulled through following his second liver transplant and we were all there to support him. Life was really hard at this time and we felt like we were on an emotional rollercoaster. My health and wellbeing had been completely neglected. I lost myself and, unknowingly, was in a state of deep postpartum depression.

The stress of everything happening seemed to take over and I began spiral out of control. At this point I was only about 180 pounds, which for my height is considered obese. I figured I would try to work out on the Wii we got our son for Christmas; he wasn't really using it and we had the Wii Fit Game that seemed like a great tool to get moving in the privacy of our own home. In my head I only needed to lose about ten to fifteen pounds, just to target my belly and I would be fine.

> IT WAS NOT UNTIL I STEPPED ON THE WII, SAW MY WEIGHT CLASSIFICATION READ OBESE, AND I SAW MY AVATAR EXPAND, THAT I REALIZED HOW MUCH I LET MYSELF GO.

I was motivated to get started and lose some weight, until one day I almost broke my ankle coming down the stairs and ended up in a boot for months; now I had an excuse not to workout. I was also prescribed prescription pain medicine, which started to become a crutch, as most addictive pharmaceutical drugs can. When I noticed that I was developing a dependency on the feeling the medicine gave me and not so much for the ankle pain, I knew I had to stop.

I was not okay mentally, emotionally, spiritually, and physically; it showed. I finally realized one day that my weight was becoming a bit out of control. I finally saw it; I looked in the mirror and I couldn't recognize myself. I especially could not stand to look at my naked body. I hadn't really acknowledge my weight gain until my daughter was about a year old and now I needed a size fourteen or larger, when I've never been bigger than a size ten or medium, and that was when I was my thickest.

So I went into a state of denial; I refused to buy any clothes over the size fourteen, even when a size fourteen no longer fit me. I tried to act as if I was satisfied with my body, when inside I was disgusted by how much I had let myself go. My husband told me he was still attracted to me and I could not believe him. I was thinking, "How could he be really physically attracted to me?" I was not attracted to myself and I definitely did not feel sexy or even pretty anymore. I hated how I looked in pictures, so I would hide anytime someone would bring out their camera. Now that I look back I have very few pictures of myself during this time and the pictures I that did take I was embarrassed to share with anyone. I masked my pain with a smile and acted like my weight did not bother me.

> FINALLY, I GOT TIRED OF WEARING TIGHT CLOTHES THAT REALLY DIDN'T FIT AND GIRDLES THAT MADE ME FEEL LIKE A STUFFED SAUSAGE. I WAS NEARLY 200 POUNDS AND A TRUE SIZE SIXTEEN TO EIGHTEEN OR EXTRA LARGE. I WAS UNHAPPY AND DISAPPOINTED WITH MYSELF AND COULD NOT UNDERSTAND WHAT HAPPENED.

I also did not know how to fix it at first. I just wanted a quick fix. I went to the store and walked up and down the aisle looking at all of the different weight loss pills and diet supplements. On two separate occasions, I bought diet drugs that I returned the following day after reading tons of articles and testimonies about the true side effects of weight loss drugs. Then I tried herbal supplements like Green Tea Extract in hopes that it would miraculously melt all my fat without me doing any of the work.

Around this time I had a toddler, I was a full-time student, housewife, and mother. Going back to college was one of the best things I ever did for my children, and myself but it was very stressful; it was so stressful that my health began to deteriorate. I began to get headaches and I was sick all of the time; catching every cold, flu, or stomach bug in the air. My hormones were completely out of control and my menstrual cycles were irregular and extremely painful. I had been suffering with sciatic nerve pain and lower back pain that would leave me almost immobile since my first miscarriage and now it was getting even worse. I would get out of the bed in the morning and fall to the floor in pain once my feet would hit the ground. Walking became scary and painful because my hips would go out of socket if I made one wrong step.

I had a serious problem digesting food. Childbirth left me with hemorrhoids, which got so bad that I was bleeding from my rectum on a daily basis. It was out of control and terrifying. After going to the hospital and seeing a gastrointestinal disease specialist it was suggested that I have a colonoscopy to rule out intestinal cancer or cyst. This was a major wake-up call for me. I was blessed that it was not something fatal or extremely serious. I found out that my problem was a fissure in my lower intestines attributed to a diet lacking enough fiber and water. My stomach would get upset every time I had a major test or paper to write or something stressful was happening at home; I felt completely broken down; I was too young to feel like this. I had too much to live for, and I was tired of being cranky and in pain, instead of running and playing with my beautiful children and enjoying my life.

The light bulb went off one day in the office of my gastrointestinal specialist. He asked me if I drank enough water and got enough fiber in my diet. My answer was no, I was not drinking enough water or eating enough fiber. It was at this moment that I realized I had the power to change my situation. I was going to school to get a degree in nursing and one of the required courses I had to take was Nutrition. While taking this course, I started to remember that my mother had given me all the tools I needed to get well when I was younger. My mom was what I called a "health nut" when I was growing up. She juiced, shopped at whole foods when she could afford it, and did olive oil cleanses, which I thought was torture. I went out and bought a juicer and a bunch of fruits and vegetables. I started reading nutrition labels and reading books on holistic health and healing. I started throwing out all the junk food we had in the house and refused to buy anything unhealthy.

I was still in a lot of pain but I knew I had to start moving if I wanted to lose weight. So I started walking at the park. I could only walk a half a mile out and back to my car when I began. It was extremely painful, but I was determined to get the weight off. I began to use my walks as a time for prayer and meditation. Each time I would walk I would go a little farther and walk a little faster. I started to set small goals for myself and each time I would achieve a goal I would set another one. One mile became three miles and the pain that had me crippled started to go away. As I walked and prayed I realized that the condition I was in was a result of the pain and baggage I carried with me throughout my life. As I began to lose weight I also started to let go of all the pain, disappointment, and resentment I was carrying.

With every pound I lost I gained my joy, peace, and happiness back. My weight loss journey inspired me to help others. I switched my major from nursing to nutrition and dietetics, got my Nutrition and Wellness Consultant Certification along with a Zumba Instructor Certification, and continued to work on improving myself in spirit, mind, and body. I kept walking and jogging in the park and one day I met my best friend and business partner Stenia. Stenia was training a friend of mine who introduced us. After the first day we met, I kept bumping into her on my walks; something in my spirit kept telling me she was someone I needed to know. I challenged myself to running a 5K in the Oklahoma Memorial Marathon and since I always saw Stenia running in the park and I knew she was a trainer, I asked her for some advice. She gave me a 5K training schedule that was designed to get me from the couch to running a 5K. My training began in January when it was severely cold outside. I found a ten-day free pass in a local newspaper to the YMCA and decided to try it out since they had an indoor track. Stenia worked at the Y and suggested I take some group exercise classes to help me train for my 5K. After my ten-day pass was up I joined the YMCA and got a family membership. I started taking a variety of group exercise classes and mentioned to one of the instructors that I was certified to teach Zumba. I got hired to be a substitute Zumba instructor and began to sub for classes. That led to a position as a Fitness Instructor working in the fitness center of the Y. Stenia and I began to develop a boot camp/ nutrition program geared towards women, wives, and mothers. Our company No Excuses OKC was born out of our desire to help women like ourselves to achieve their health and wellness goals through boot camp workouts, nutrition programs, and fitness parties. I have continued working at the YMCA and am now the Health and Wellness Coordinator for the Midwest City, Ok branch. Every day I get to help other people on their paths to living happier and healthier lives. I even volunteer as a soccer coach for the Y, coaching my children and others. My journey to healing myself has led me to my mission and purpose in life. Today I am happy, healthy, and able to do things physically I never thought was possible when I first started. Most importantly I am a healthy example for my children and will be around to help them navigate through life.

Jennifer Armstrong
Certified Nutrition and Wellness Consultant, Nutritionist
No Excuses OKC
(405) 593-6923
jdawnarmstrong@gmail.com

Biography of Jennifer Armstrong

Jennifer Armstrong is a Certified Nutrition and Wellness Consultant and Nutritionist, with an Associates of Arts Degree in Enterprise Development. She works part-time as a fitness instructor at the Midwest City YMCA and enjoys volunteering as a Youth Soccer Coach. She is working on obtaining a B.S. in Nutrition and Dietetics from the University of Central Oklahoma. She is the "Eat Clean" half of No Excuses OKC, along with personal trainer and exercise specialist Stenia Little. Her passion is to help other women and children live healthy, happy lives through nutrition education, fitness, and total mind, body, and spirit wellness.

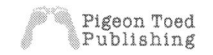

Carlie Carpio

Founder of
RegularGirlFitness

GETTING FIT IN EVERY FACET OF LIFE: HOW GETTING HEALTHY CHANGED MY LIFE AND SET ME UP FOR SUCCESS
By Carlie Carpio

What is self-love?

Nowadays you hear and see the term "self-love" everywhere all the time. It has become a social media buzzword and is the focus of so many blogs, television shows, magazine articles, etc. But what is it really? What does self-love really mean? And why does it matter? Also, since this is a book on business, what in the heck does self-love have to do with business?

be YOUtiful

First let's start with what it is.

Self-love is defined in the dictionary as having "regard for one's well-being and happiness." My personal definition doesn't deviate too far from that, I just want to add "to know that you are enough just as you are and to love yourself exactly as you are." Self-love involves casting off societal norms and standards for what you should look like, what you should be doing, and who you should be. Instead of punishing yourself when you fall short of those ridiculous standards just loving, appreciating, and being who you are and how you are. Realizing that your value is not tied to what you do or how you look. It is knowing that you are worthy just as you are.

That's great, but why does it actually matter?

It matters to me personally for a multitude of reasons, which we'll get to, but let's see what the experts have to say first. If you look through any prominent texts in business or religion, or through any research of successful people in almost any field or industry, there is one common thread: the mindset and acknowledgement of self.

"As a man thinketh so is he"
Proverbs 23:7

"You've got to be sure of self before you can ever win a prize" Napoleon Hill in *Think and Grow Rich*

"If you don't ever conquer self, you will be conquered by self" Napoleon Hill in *Think and Grow Rich*

"Man is made by his belief. As he believes, so he is"
The Bhagavad Gita

Conquering self, being sure of yourself, and having control of your mind all rest in how you feel about yourself and what you think of yourself. In this area, life and success are one in the same. They all depend on how you perceive yourself, what you believe about yourself, and what you speak about and to yourself. This all ties directly into body image and self-love because both of these begin in the mind. Self-love is a mindset and determines how you live your life. What we think and feel radiates out of us and permeates into every area of our lives. Sure you can be relatively successful without it, but I truly believe you will never be able to reach your full potential until you learn to love yourself.

"Change your thoughts, change your world"
Norman Vincent Peale

How you see yourself, how you feel about yourself, and how you think about yourself determine every aspect of your life. Your thoughts and mindset really do determine the quality of your life. Self-love is a revolution and learning how to love myself changed my life. It was only through my personal journey to get fit and feel better about myself that I realized how intertwined self-love is with the base of every other aspect of my life, especially business.

My journey with body image and self-love actually formed the basis for my company Regular Girl Fitness. Regular Girl Fitness is a movement to empower people to get healthy and fit in every area of their life and to chase their dreams. It is my blueprint for how to build a sustainable life that is healthy and feels good to you and serves to inspire others that you can get fit, love yourself, have fun, eat good food, and have a life too. Self-love affects how you think, how you feel, and how you communicate with others. Knowledge and love of self are the foundation for not just your business, but your life. This realization is relatively new in my life, but it literally changed the trajectory of my life.

Let's take this back to the beginning.

> I WAS FIRST INTRODUCED TO THE CONCEPT OF SELF-LOVE IN AN ESSENCE INTERVIEW WITH JADA PINKETT-SMITH AND WILL SMITH.

They were asking her the usual celebrity interview questions about

125

how her and Will make their relationship work. The essence of her response was basically self-love and self-care. She said that she focuses on herself first, then her relationship with her husband, and then her kids. There was some media backlash about how could she put herself before her kids, but she responded something like if "I don't take care of myself first, how can I take care of anything else?" While it outraged some, it actually made sense to me. This was a completely new concept to me, someone who was raised to always think of others before myself, and it really got me thinking. Thinking and taking action are two completely different things however. Although I understood why she said this and it made an impact on me, the development of this mentality, and actually learning to love myself and putting it into action in my life would not come until much later.

Why self-love matters to me.

Cue later. I've always been a relatively fit, athletic, and competitive person. I've been an athlete for as long as I can remember. From the time I was little, I played almost every sport you can imagine: soccer, volleyball, track, basketball, dance, color guard, flag football, martial arts, and the list goes on. That drive and ambition infused all the other areas of my life and became my way of life. Whenever I got to college however, all of that changed. I no longer had the team sports to keep me engaged and active. I went from having year round team workouts, tournaments, and games, to actively seeking out going to the gym for solo "workouts." Boy, was this a culture shock for me. Not only was I dealing with the absence of a team to belong to, but also losing the consistency of sports keeping my mind and body disciplined and in shape. Which was a double whammy. Running and trying to lift with the limited knowledge I'd gained in sports over the years didn't quite generate the results I was used to.

I would run and run, and tried to lift weights, played intramural sports, and did every active competition I could. Still, it was never enough. I started to get a little discouraged. Then, I had what my mentor would call a "life-interrupted moment." This is an event that occurs that initiates or forces change in your life. Well, mine happened in the form of an ACL tear. Which for anyone who has ever had that surgery and painful, restrictive recovery process – it is a complete nightmare. I was miserable. On top of that I lost a family member who was very close to me. This combination sent me over the edge and I had a breakdown. I gained so much weight, began to withdraw from my very active and social life, and became depressed and down. It got to a point where I didn't even recognize myself in the mirror. Not just physically, but my spirit seemed different. The fire in my eyes wasn't as bright. How did I ever allow myself to get to this point?

I was there for a while, feeling unhappy and stuck. Something had to change, but what? How? Clearly what I was doing wasn't working. I began making consistent, conscious choices and changes to my nutrition and workouts. I took a nutrition class and I also had some encouragement and the support of some really good friends. Slowly, I started moving and shaking again. I had gotten a good bit of the extra weight off, but more importantly I started feeling like myself again. The fog was clearing, I was getting back in the groove, and I liked what I saw when I looked in the mirror. I had done it! I won! Go me!!! Getting physically fit had solved my issues. Or so I thought…

Fast forward to a year later. I had another "life-interrupted moment" when dealing with a break-up and some family issues and I began to lose myself again. I was very physically fit by this point, but oddly enough this didn't make it any better. Even though I was fit, I still didn't feel good about myself or frankly, anything else. With my old formula, physical fitness had been my solution, but now? I just wasn't happy with where I was.

That's when I realized that it wasn't just the decline in my physical health and fitness that made me feel down or depressed. It added to the situation, I'm certain, but it wasn't the root cause of the issue. It also wasn't just liking the way I looked that made me feel good. I was trying to get out of this rut, but I felt stuck. I knew something was missing. Physical health and fitness were a key contributing factor for what made me feel better and pulled me up the first time, why was this time any different?

Although I know physical fitness was an important factor to getting out of my funk and feeling better about myself, there were so many other things in my life and inside myself that I had to deal with. Physically I was good, but there was an array of other areas of my life that weren't healthy or fit. My mentor encouraged me to start journaling, practicing self-love, and to maybe even go see a counselor. I did all of those, and so much more.

This is the part of health that is the not so fun or flashy. This is the type of stuff that people don't care to talk about. In fact, these are the things that people purposely avoid talking about. The tough stuff; the part beyond the physical body. It's easy to discuss meal plans and the latest workout trends or the newest craze in supplements, diets, or bright new workout gear, but as soon as you bring up mental, emotional, or spiritual health people get antsy and uncomfortable. They completely shut down.

It's crazy, and extremely infuriating, that we live in a society when these topics are still so taboo to discuss. Body-wise? Great! Let's get fit! Everybody loves to talk about bodies, measuring up, weight loss, and muscle progress. Emotions or mental health though? Nah, let's not. Honestly, the mind, spirit, and emotions are the hardest parts of fitness to deal with. What most people, myself included, usually don't realize is that you can't be truly successful with one area if you don't work on the others. How can we truly have a good body image when we don't take care of every part of our bodies?

Think of your body as a well-designed machine. The mind, body, and soul, (and subsequently self-love, body image, and mindset) are all parts of the same machine. Let's say this machine is an automobile. A car is a complex mechanism with lots of pieces and parts that all fit and work together to produce optimal performance. We are fearfully and wonderfully made enigmas with tons of parts that intricately go and work together. If one piece is broken, it can throw off the entire system. Only working out one part of your body, for example just your physical fitness is like paying attention to only one part of your car. Which is completely nonsensical. You wouldn't only wash the outside of your car for upkeep and maintenance. You have to put gas in it, maintain the engine, air up the tires, get oil changes, regular checkups, etc. So why do we typically only focus on one area when it comes to ourselves? Then we wonder why nothing else is working or why things don't sustainably get better?

I never realized how much health affected my life on a broader scale until I struggled with it. Your health and fitness determine your success in business and in life. And no, I'm not just talking about having abs and a nice booty. Which is nice, and can help some things. I mean being fit in every area of your life: mind, body, and soul. It wasn't until I started getting fit in every facet of my life that the pieces began to fit together and I was able to really connect to my passions. It was only through total health and self-love that these opportunities came about. Self-love opened up so many doors. It was like a whole new world where I realized I could do anything and actually enjoy my life. Sometimes I still can't believe how great I can feel and how happy I can be. It's like getting glasses with the right prescription for the first time. These doors couldn't be opened however, until I worked on myself from the inside out.

So I started working on myself. All of those shameful and uncomfortable parts. Slowly and painfully I moved forward working on all of me. Not just select pieces, but all of me. Together. Guess what happened when I did? Magic. It was like things just started clicking. I started Regular Girl Fitness to help chronicle my journey into fitness. I actually made a separate Instagram account for it because I didn't want people to get sick of seeing my fitness posts. So I started posting. The next thing I knew, I had 300 followers, then 500, then 1500, and it's still growing. All I was doing was posting my personal journey and struggles with self-love, fitness, inspiration, and nutrition. I was keeping track of my journey, but in turn started inspiring others. That's when I realized I had a passion for helping others reach their goals and decided to get certified as a personal trainer.

Now I'm working on getting a yoga teaching certification, speaking at health and fitness conferences, blogging, and hosting retreats for both fitness and self-love. They go hand in hand. I would have never gotten here if it were not for people like my mentor in my life encouraging me to start that self-love journey. Now that I'm on it, there's no looking back. Not only did I gain confidence, self-love, and opportunities to explore my passions, I also lost some stuff. All of this guilt, shame, negativity, and emotional baggage I didn't even know I was carrying have been melting away since the day I started down this path.

Learning how to love myself was the first step to sustainable health and fitness. It all comes down to your mind. The first question I had to ask myself and now the first one I ask my clients is:

"Why are you doing this?"

"Why do you want to get fit?"

"What's your motivation?" closely followed by

"So, what are your goals?"

More often than not, the foundation of their reasoning for getting fit is negative. I know you're probably wondering – how can wanting and working towards getting fit be negative? Although it brings about positive effects on your body and psyche, it doesn't solve the problem. If you start anything with a negative intention your output will never be positive. For example, if you decide to work out because you hate your body or hate the way you look or feel about yourself – working out alone won't change that. You will never be happy with how you look. Your results will never be enough and you will still be negative and extremely hard on yourself. It isn't the actual physical manifestation that is the issue; the root of the problem is in your mind. It's your perspective and how you're viewing everything.

Self-love isn't reliant upon you fitting into your dream size jeans. Self-love means loving yourself just as you are. Yes, exactly as you are and working to be the best, happiest, most fulfilled version of yourself. Choosing and doing what is best for you – which include getting healthy! So the first step to getting fit in every facet in life is to figure out your foundation. If it lies in something negative, I implore you to dig a little deeper and forge forward on a positive reason. Instead of working out because you hate your body, work out because you love yourself and want to be the best possible version of yourself. Self-love isn't settling for anything, it's about owning your power to choose to do what's best for you and accepting that you are enough as is.

> FITNESS IS SO MUCH MORE THAN JUST ABS. HEALTH IS SO MUCH MORE THAN YOUR WORKOUTS OR WHAT YOU EAT.

Although all of that is vitally important, your mind and spirit have to be right to or its all for naught. This goes with anything in life, not just fitness. Make sure your mindset and self-love foundation are strong, and then move forward with your goal setting. Once you have your foundation established, what are your goals? What is your intention? What do you want to accomplish?

My goal was to learn to love myself and to be the best possible version of myself. Getting fit in every facet of my life changed me. Not only did I discover a new passion, I actually found myself. I got to know me, love me, respect me, and began to work on every area of my life. This led to more breakthroughs than you can imagine in every possible area of my life! This happened with fitness, and me but it could be any career, any industry. Since I've started my journey I have changed careers, went back to school, and manifested old and new dreams and goals. When you feel better about you – the way you look, think, act, even the way you carry yourself changes. It all starts with mindset and self-love, but the possibilities from there are limitless!

beYOUtiful

Let's start a self-love revolution.

Self-love and a healthy body image are a revolution because it goes against everything that society and the public teaches us. Any and everywhere you look there are things telling us that we are too fat, too skinny, not tall enough, not curvy enough, not smart enough, not accomplished enough, not well traveled, not where we are supposed to be in general. Just all the way around – not enough. Everything in life is challenging us to become more, get better, do more, and buy more. All of this is fine, but not if we don't first realize that we are whole and worthy without any of these things.

It's not an easy journey, but it is most definitely worth it. We all struggle with this daily, and I am no exception. It is still a choice every day. There is so much power in acknowledging this and deciding to move forward.

One of the best things about self-love?

It's contagious!

Watch how you lifting up you and inspiring yourself brings up those around you. It's a win-win-win. For you, your business, and those in your lives. So do it for you, yourself, and your business! Do it for your future!

Let self-love and a renewed mindset rebuild you and your brand from the inside out.

Biography of Carlie Caprio

Carlie is a graduate student, yogi, certified personal trainer, foodie, traveler, an avid reader, and a lover of life. She founded RegularGirlFitness when she realized that she was unhappy and had not been making her health a priority. RGF serves as a chronicle of her journey and to inspire others, as well as herself, that you can get healthy, stay fit, and still have a life too. Fitness isn't just about the abs, it's about being fit in every facet of your life.

Elizabeth Reeve

Founder of
Ms. Abilities America

Today's American Woman
National Elegant Mrs. 2015;
Ms. Wheelchair Oklahoma
(America) 2008-2009;
Ms. Wheelchair Oklahoma
(USA) 2011-2012;
Ms. Pageant Gal Hope
Princess 2014;
Ms. Service Dog Angel
Lifetime Queen

MORE THAN ABLE:
THE POWER IN ALLOWING ONE'S ABILITIES TO GUIDE THE JOURNEY
By Elizabeth Reeve

The most beautiful and intricate moments in life are often appreciated long after that part of your journey has ended and you are able to look back and simply say, "Wow." More often, those are the whispers of greatness God has allowed to propel you to your next level… but as you experience each, they can seem like the most difficult, painful and gut-wrenching moments to overcome.

be YOUtiful

A person's life changes over time. Some individuals struggle with change, while others navigate a safe path through every struggle. If we are careful to consider the turns and curves as we experience them, we will find – though very difficult, they are the keys that unlock doors to our most valuable abilities and attributes. Instead of looking at every we reason we can't do something, we should look at every reason we can! When one concentrates on their abilities instead of their disabilities, they will become more successful and love every aspect of life. This is a trait I have embraced and utilized to live a life that I love, appreciate and thrive to grow in. From a very young age, I learned the power in allowing my abilities to guide my journey.

> When I was a young lady, I had difficulties with eye-to-hand coordination. The doctors were worried that my vision and responsive action may never function as expected.

I know my parents and grandparents were concerned about this disability. They could have given up. They could have told me that I was unable to be successful… simply accepting what the doctors said. However, my grandfather, Rayful D. Sears, was unwilling to accept the diagnosis! He went out to the woodshop and created a board that had screws on it. He wanted to make sure I had something I could work on and develop proper hand-to-eye coordination. My family worked tirelessly for what seemed like a million hours to help me develop those skills. This was the foundation of my success - one I am very grateful for.

My father was in the military, for a time we lived in Germany. In Germany, I was in the first grade. My sister loved a teacher by the name of Mrs. Olsen, I asked to be put in her class! I learned slowly. I also struggled during social interactions. I often would stand aside and do things in different ways… far different from my peers. I wasn't a social butterfly and struggled with this throughout life. My peers would make fun of everything about me, from my speech impediment to my awkward appearance. I had an overbite, also known as buck teeth. I was made fun of and bullied. I could have given up and decided that my disabilities were too great, but this caused me to try harder.

One day, I was in the playground, playing on the monkey bars. I really enjoyed doing flips. I was often alone and that was ok for me. One of the girls in my class decided to come up and yell at me. She told me to get off the monkey bars, because she wanted to play on them. There was another set of monkey bars right next us… she could have played on them. I refused to make a move. So, she bit me. I decided to bite her back. She went to Mrs. Olsen and told her I bit her. Mrs. Olsen called me over. She looked at me and said, "Rabid Dog!" When the class went inside, I was separated from the rest of the class and they called my mother to come and get me. This was one of many bullying incidents I endured in elementary school.

In third grade, my family moved back to Texas. School was difficult. I suffered because of my unique linguistic skills and my inability to understand most of the learning material in class. The school administration and my parents decided it would be best to place me back in second grade. It was frustrating because on top of that my peers would continue to make fun of my appearance. I did my best to avoid others and concentrate on my studies. However, it was very difficult being a slow learner. I had to make a choice not to allow the overt opinions of my peers to control how I considered and interacted with others. I chose to concentrate on the good things in life. I acknowledged my beautiful abilities that other students did not have, which allowed me to powerfully change my life in positive ways. I grew to become a brilliantly positive, grateful person, maturely focusing on my abilities, instead of my disabilities. I still had difficulties doing what other students were able to do… activities most people take for granted, like running. However, I was blessed to meet other individuals who suffered from similar disabilities to my own. One individual became my role model, Kristina. Kristina was a child who had severe disabilities. She was unable to do many things. She had to be spoon fed, could not walk and needed help with daily living skills. Kristina was non-verbal. Her life was an amazing example and made a huge impact on how I viewed life. I spent many hours with Kristina and we became the best of friends.

Kristina was the first example on how one should consider what they could do in life, rather than focus on what they could not do. Kristina became the motivation to how I perceived my future. Elizabeth learned to love swimming, doing circus acts, and learning to give of herself to others. When I was bullied, I would always know I could go down to Kristina's house. I enjoyed hanging out with Kristina. I didn't see Kristina's disabilities, but instead saw Kristina's ability to be a friend and to love. I did not see the fact Kristina was in a wheelchair, or that she couldn't do things in a normal way… or anything negative, for that matter. I saw the love and care Kristina had to give to others. She was my best friend.

> THEN, MY FAMILY MOVED BACK TO GERMANY. IN GERMANY, I GOT BRACES, BUT I ALSO HAD TO START WEARING GLASSES. MY PEERS WOULD CALL ME TIN MOUTH AND FOUR EYES.

I loved the opportunity to experience different cultures. Some cultures were certainly nicer than others. That's when I began to focus more on my abilities in math, reading, and writing. Mr. Smith, the band director, enjoyed having me in his class, because I was persistent and overlooked the negativity of my peers. The definition of my body image came from within, instead of looking at the superficial outside.

At the end of the year, Mr. Smith asked me to come to his advanced band class. He knew I had problems playing the instrument due to eye-to-hand coordination, and that I would only focus on the positive to accept my abilities instead of my disabilities. The other students started to laugh at how I played the flute. Mr. Smith made the students stop laughing, and focus on the fact that everyone has some weakness and we all need to focus on what we can do rather than what we cannot do. For the first time, I realized how I could make a positive impact on others despite my disabilities.

In the eighth grade, my sister and I moved to Oklahoma to live with my Grandmother and uncle. I found out there were some major differences between what I knew and what American children knew. I had hung out with German children more than American children. I was different and still very innocent. In Oklahoma, children knew about weed, marijuana, and other things I was unfamiliar with. They made fun of me because I didn't understand that birds and the bees, as well as things that occur when you become a woman. I hated school. Once, I tried to throw myself down the stairs at school to hurt myself. It didn't work and I knew it was the wrong thing to do. My parents were still in Germany, and I couldn't go back there because it was a bad environment due to the bombings going on at the time.

When my parents finally moved back to the states, we moved to Tahlequah. I tried to fit in. I tried to be something I wasn't and it proved to be a mistake. I wanted my peers to believe I was an athlete and could do whatever they did. I didn't want anyone to know how weak I was and how much I hurt every time I tried to run. But, I ran with a twist. I really wanted to encourage those watching to keep going… but they laughed at me and their laughter was louder than my confidence. Louder than my courage… and louder than my leadership. I ended up on crutches with ankles swollen and twisted. I never understood why I was so slow. However, later in life I was told that I suffered from minimal spinal bifida, which is why I could walk, but in a limited way.

They recognized I was trying to blend in and would make fun of me. It became my life story in a way… people making fun of me… if not for one thing another. They would talk about me because of my culture, for not shaving my legs, the way I dressed, and the way I saw the world.

I was fortunate to have several great educators who helped me realize I needed to be me… the authentic me. My teachers taught me to overlook what I couldn't do and focus on what I could do. They believed in me!

Mr. Price was the band director. I wanted to be in band with my sister. It was very difficult because of my hand-to-eye coordination... not to mention it was a marching band. I was always getting out of step, trying to play the same instrument as my sister; I wanted to be exactly like her! In my eyes, she was a better me... an ideal me. Mr. Price saw what was happening, and started working with me to teach her to be myself. I was able to do some things with the band, but again it was limited. Mr. Price taught me to consider what my life would be like if I would focus on my strengths. My sister was great at playing instruments, but I had strength in academics.

Mrs. Rader was my English teacher. She understood me. Many of the frustrations I felt started to appear in my writing. I would often concentrate on drop outs, how educators needed to take a stronger responsibility of individuals who wanted to drop out of school, and making students stay in a school where they could be more accountable for their education. The sarcasm in my writing would be revealed. I was accused by one of my teachers of plagiarism and was embarrassed in front of my classmates, which caused more difficulties with my peers. Mrs. Rader helped me to see how my writings could improve. Mrs. Rader was a positive role model and left a lasting impact on my attitude toward life.

When it came to challenging students, Mr. Crawford was one who would not settle for laziness or choosing to do a project less than he knew I was capable of. I remember, I tried to do a science fair project dealing with fleas on dogs. Mr. Crawford encouraged me to focus on the genetics of rabbits. He understood I was discouraged due to being accused of plagiarism; however, he knew if I wasn't pushed to think on a higher scale, I would give up. I wanted to become a veterinarian; he knew the study of genetics would encourage me to think on a higher level and possibly follow my dream.

I dropped out of band to follow my dream of becoming a veterinarian. I loved animals! I worked with animals in Future Farmers of America. But, again I was bullied. This was a reoccurring theme and like a never-ending nightmare. The FFA teacher, Mr. Stinnett decided I should focus on speaking and writing. Mr. Stinnett gave me the unique opportunity to research different topics and write papers based upon my findings. This was an opportunity not many other students were able to take advantage of and it was truly perfect! Dr. Smith, the tenth grade English teacher, encouraged I increase development in my writing skills. If I didn't put forth enough effort, she would make me redo the work. I learned to hand in work acceptable of my performance and capabilities the first time! Dr. Smith truly helped me to fall in love with education and attending school. Even when I got the flu and my temperature was over 100 degrees, I did not want to miss school due because I couldn't wait to talk to Dr. Smith. Dr. Smith encouraged me to take Honors English in the eleventh grade.

By the time I was in Junior year, I was enrolled in Speech, Drama, and Honors English. I loved to compete in speech competitions. I often received third place in competitions. Clearly, my strength was extemporaneous speaking. I overcome my inability to speak at a younger age to master the art of giving full speeches by my teenage years. It was amazing! I could have given in to the bullying, instead, I allowed the bullying to make me stronger. I managed my remaining disabilities, but I really began to shine a bright light and focus in on my strengths.

Unfortunately, Senior year, I had to move and was not accepted well in the new school. This is what I expected. I just couldn't shake the feeling that everything I had worked was starting to prove worthless and fruitless. I was even put down by my English and Speech teachers. I was forced to enroll in physical education, where I was called fat and slow. I felt as though someone had firmly affixed a label to my clothing that read, "inferior." For the first time in high school, I was given detention and forced into realizing that my disability was unaccepted by most. Later, I had an accident on the trampoline and injured my neck and knee to the point of needing orthoscopic surgery. Everything seemed to flip upside down. Instead of focusing on my abilities, I found myself focused on my inabilities again.

During my first year of college, my dream of becoming a veterinarian went away due to my struggles with biology and inability to overcome my self-esteem issues. I had the opportunity of working in the greenhouse with the botany department, which caused me to lose feeling in my hand due to trying to save the plants with an unknown chemical coming up the sink. I almost failed school with a GPA of 1.49.

Transferring to another university would prove to be a necessary step for me to continue to try and excel. I transferred to Tarleton State University. During my Biology class, I would run into Michelle Bostock Parish. The first day of class, Michelle came in and asked if she could sit down next to me. I told Michelle there was a seat across the room, due to the way Michelle looked. Michelle had some defects on her face, and I was in denial because of my own disabilities. I believed if I allowed Michelle to get close, I would have to accept my own disabilities. Michelle was determined to find out why I was being the way I was. Michelle started a long-standing friendship with me that continues even today. Due to the determination of Michelle, I would go on to make progress and accept my disabilities while I focused on my abilities. I obtained my Bachelor of Arts in History. In 1998, my father encouraged me to take on a first-grade position. I had not taken any early childhood education classes. With the inexperience and lack of self-esteem, I would not be successful in the position. However, I obtained my post-baccalaureate degree in Elementary education. I obtained my teaching degree in Special Education, English as a second language, and Elementary 1-8. I became a special education teacher in a severe and profound classroom.

In 2000, I was given the scare of possibly having lymphoma. I had a biopsy, which came back as sarcoid. Sarcoid is the growth of tiny collections of inflammatory cells in different parts of your body — most commonly the lungs, lymph nodes, eyes and skin. This sarcoid has spread into my other organs as time has passed.

In 2001, I was positioning one of my students who had severe disabilities and happened to have epilepsy. The student started to have a seizure. I had to decide to either drop the student and take a chance of injuring the student or get the student to the ground and take a chance of injuring myself. I took the chance of injuring myself, which caused a spinal cord injury. I was still able to walk at this point, but this was when things began to decline and eventually prevented my walking on a permanent basis. Due to the inability to lift again, I had to resign from the position. The next position was a life skills position. Unfortunately, I was unable to keep the student's safe because I was not able to help the students with their disabilities. In 2005, I and my husband decided to move to where I could get more medical attention in order to try to help me maintain my ability to walk. However, the move proved to not help and I would be placed in a wheelchair. I was found to have spinal bifida, spinal cord injury, and MS. I had to look at the lifetime of being in a wheelchair. This was not what I wanted to hear, and I felt like life was at an end. I started seeing my health decline, right as my life had reached a pentacle. I had fought all of my life and everything seemed like it was time to give up. I did not see anything positive coming out of being in a wheelchair.

Living close to a university, I decided to try and get a business degree. I loved working on computers and saw an opportunity to work from home once I obtained my degree. I entered the university with the help of vocational rehabilitation. I had the pleasure to meet Dr. Renee Cambiano and Dr. Ernest Bekerring. Although many other professors tried to boost my self-esteem, these two professors spent time encouraging me to become the very best I could become. Dr. Bekerring helped show me that I had the ability of doing research on a higher level. Dr. Renee Cambiano kept my dream of being an educator alive. Through their persistence, I graduated with my BBA in Information Systems.

During the time within my studies, I was introduced to the opportunities to serve on the IDEA Part B board. This was an opportunity where I could learn more about what was happening on the state level of Education within the state of Oklahoma. This encouraged me to think about trying to go back into the classroom and teach. However, I had to discover how to continue and learn the information to make sure I would be able to help the students.

In 2008, I was given the opportunity go to Ms. Wheelchair America as Ms. Wheelchair Oklahoma. This was an opportunity I never thought would be possible. I had heard of Miss America and Miss USA, but never any pageants for those who were older. I decided to research what was required to enter the pageant. While at the pageant, I went through workshops on different issues of being in a wheelchair and saw positive role models in wheelchairs. I learned my life did not come to an end when placed in a wheelchair. I learned about service dogs and how they could help with mobility. This was a turning point as I began to believe I could make a difference in the lives of others, despite being in a wheelchair.

Upon returning home, I began to research how to obtain a service dog and what it would look like to have a service dog help me cope day-to-day with my disabilities. I loved dogs and thought about how wonderful it would be to have a dog help encourage me with my daily activities. I wondered if having a service dog would allow me to blossom and have a better life. I placed my research in a book, so others would not have to repeat the same research if they should also want the ability to have a service dog. The book was entitled ADA and You: Service Dogs.

I then became the state director for Ms. Wheelchair Oklahoma. During my term as the state director, I encouraged many individuals to become the best they could. However, I felt I wanted to explore other avenues. I resigned as the state director to explore Ms. Wheelchair USA. I continued to have interests and began learning how to found a new pageant system. I was unsure how to go about creating the pageant, but knew I wanted to give everyone with visible and invisible disabilities the opportunity to experience the pageant. In 2011, I started to form Ms. Abilities America. The pageant was to allow individuals to advocate for many individuals who happen to have disabilities, lead by example, and mentor those who have just begun their journey towards finding their abilities, while showing friendship to all individuals and achieving to their best through academics and beyond in the ever-growing world. I researched how to turn this idea into a national pageant. I knew I needed to make it within a reasonable cost for individuals who were on social security, yet make it for those who would become positive role models to many. I understood this would be a work in progress for many years, as I wanted to make it a pageant where others would come into the desire to want to compete within the pageant.

Then I began having problems training my own service dog. I took my dog to Marjorie Shatterfield. Marjorie decided to start a service dog training program, Glad Wags. Sassy became one of my first service dogs. Under Ms. Abilities America, Glad Wags has become a nonprofit. I could assist many other individuals to obtain service dogs through the use of putting my 501-C3 into action.
I continued to do my research on pageantry by entering other pageants. I learned about being given titles to perform work on causes, competing in various pageants, and how the ins and outs of pageantry can be beneficial to one's self-esteem. However, one must learn to be more social and learn how to keep quiet to some of the individuals within the business. I learned pageantry is a business to some, while being a community service to others. It has taught me to take on various causes called platforms. I began to see myself more as an individual and not as someone in a wheelchair.

In 2012, I obtained my Masters in Special Education. I moved from Tahlequah to Oklahoma City to try working within a classroom once again. However, this would prove to be a mistake as I was unable to help the students remain safe within the emotionally disturbed classroom. I wanted to help the students, but I felt it was necessary to make sure the students could stay safe. Without being able to answer honestly to myself, to the parents and to the administration the students would remain safe, I resigned from the position. At this point, I had to answer the question of whether it would be possible for an individual in a wheelchair to be a positive role model within a classroom. At first, I wanted to answer no, but then I began to consider the possibility of higher education.

I began to work on my doctorate. At first, I wanted to focus on Special Education. However, I soon focused the work more on developing Ms. Abilities America, Inc. I understood there was more work to be done and wanted to focus on creating a more positive environment to help others discover how they could exemplify their abilities over their disabilities. I understood the need to make the organization become a 501-c3, and do what it was created to do. In January 2012, Ms. Abilities America became a 501-c3.

I decided it was best to try and help the ladies understand what was expected of them within the pageant. I wanted them to have successful reigns. The first couple of ladies who have been Ms. Abilities Americas have proven to be role models. Within the pageant, they can see themselves for their abilities and not their disabilities. I wanted to set the bar higher for my titleholders, so I have entered other pageants as well. I refused to put the non-compete clause on my ladies, as that would defeat the purpose of Ms. Abilities America.

In 2014, I started teaching English as a second language at a local community college. I have completed one year of instruction and was able to begin a second year. I have worked to help increase the way my students perceive themselves by giving them opportunities such as being published in a book produced for those who are in the ESL and GED programs in higher education. I have also helped them give back to the community through projects such as the Pet Food Pantry, which gives to those who have disabilities, homeless, or elderly.

I entered Todays American Woman as Elegant Mrs. Oklahoma. While at the pageant, I was given the Spirit of Pageantry and the Presidents Gold Community Service Award. I have had the opportunity to do things I never thought possible with disabilities. I have run 5Ks in my wheelchair with my service dog including the OKC Memorial Marathon, which is in honor of those who lost their lives during the Oklahoma City bombings. Other runs I have participated in include Oklahoma City New Year's Day 5K, Oklahoma City 5K finale, and Tulsa Jingle Run. I have been appointed by the Governor of Oklahoma to be on the State

Independent Living Council and Oklahoma Rehabilitation Council. In 2015, I was given the opportunity to become Todays American Woman National Elegant Mrs. During my reign, I could go to Washington DC to advocate for those who have disabilities and Virginia Beach to learn more about advocacy efforts. Unfortunately, I stepped away from Todays American Woman after being crowned as the National Elegant Mrs.

I was given the honor to continue my platform in American Majestics, as Ms. Diversity Oklahoma. I have moved forward with my platforms to include anti-bullying, anti-cyberbullying, rescue animals, and abilities over disabilities. I continued to work on my dissertation to complete my Doctorate of Education in Organizational Leadership. I could go to Phoenix, Arizona and to Columbus, Ohio. In April, I will be competing for Nationals in the American Majestics pageant. I will be helping many organizations work towards their 501-c3 status in the future. I have learned how to do virtual runs and extended the opportunity to others to help do fundraisers for their organizations.

I could have turned at any time and given up based upon my body image and my disabilities. I could have decided the bullying was too much to endure. Life has not been an easy task for me from the time I was young. I have had many obstacles, been made to see myself in a negative light, and forced to face myself in the mirror of life. At any time, I could have thrown in the towel and not allowed myself to see what would happen next in life. I came close many times, and I did consider giving up at times. So many times, I wondered why I had to go through the obstacles, the trials and the tears. One does not understand why things happen in life, but through each turn of life came a new lesson for me to learn for my future goals. From having an overbite to being placed in a wheelchair, I learned there were other individuals who had harder struggles than I. Other individuals have had the opportunity to learn from what I have gone through in life. In life, everyone is a time piece of inspiration. The purpose of life is not to be here for oneself, but to be useful for others. It is to give of oneself, one's talents, one's heart and one's service. When one learns to give of themselves in service, heart, and mind, the individual truly finds their abilities over their disabilities. They can live their life to the fullest when they turn their minds from the can'ts to the cans, and give to their community and to others. I have learned to be who I am by looking at what I can do and by giving to others through the visions of the cans.

Biography of Elizabeth Reeves

Elizabeth Reeve is Today's American Woman National Elegant Mrs. 2015. She is the founder of Ms. Abilities America, Ms. Wheelchair Oklahoma (America) 2008-2009, Ms. Wheelchair Oklahoma (USA) 2011-2012, Ms. Pageant Gal Hope Princess 2014, and Ms. Service Dog Angel Lifetime Queen. Through pageantry, she wants to help the public understand how disabilities do not make an individual, but instead the abilities. Her second platform is promoting rescuing shelter animals and providing them the homes they deserve.

Mrs. Reeve is currently working on her EdD at Grand Canyon University. She has a Master's degree in Special Education from Western Governors University, Bachelors of Business Administration from Northeastern State University, and Bachelors of Arts in History from Tarleton State University. She attended Texas Christian University for her Post-Baccalaureate teaching credentials to become certified in Texas and Oklahoma for English as a Second language, Special Education, and Elementary 1-8.

Mrs. Reeve is currently working at Oklahoma City Community College as an English as a Second Language instructor. She has written three books on service dogs, and assisted many of her students in becoming published authors.

No matter what type of path one might walk on or the journey one might be taking in life, there are always individuals who look up to one. It is within the journey, one should consider their abilities and not their disabilities through all they accomplish.

Nina Ellis-Hervey

Ph.D., L.P., N.C.S.P., L.S.S.P., C.P.C.
Licensed Psychologist #37316
Licensed Specialist in School Psychology #70264
Certified Professional Life Coach
Associate Professor
School Psychology Assessment Center Director
School Psychology Program
Human Services
Stephen F. Austin State University

THE UTILIZATION OF SOCIAL MEDIA TO INCREASE SELF-ESTEEM AND ALLEVIATE THE OBESITY EPIDEMIC IN MULTICULTURAL WOMEN

By Nina Ellis-Hervey, PhD, LSSP, NCSP

Over the years, many multicultural women have become social activists by utilizing their popularity platforms to create pertinent change in various areas of concern. One such area is fitness and obesity. Many articles highlight activists such as First Lady Michelle Obama, who focuses on alleviating the obesity epidemic in childhood through such initiatives as her "Let's Move" campaign, which pushes citizens to question healthier eating and exercise habits (Haupt, 2013). Many multicultural women activists focused on changing issues of obesity, more specifically in multicultural communities, seem to face various criticisms. These include the constant reminder of myths, which appear to be geared at the continuance of ignorance related to multicultural women and their positive gains in personal accountability, related to fitness and health. One such myth cited several times is the avoidance of fitness-related activities by multicultural women due to vanity and preserving of high maintenance hair practices (Hall et al., 2013). However, many social activists in the blogosphere and various platforms prove such myths wrong and continually make more multicultural women aware of positive fitness initiatives and everyday ways to make their lives healthier and happier.

A small, but ever extending body of research within psychology and education has explored the context of popular culture as a means to educate diverse populations (McLeod, 2007; Walker, 2006). According to the American Heart Association (2012), "Healthcare providers should embrace its [social media] potential as a tool for promoting healthy behavioral change" (para. 2). Social media and networks appear to be quite influential tools, more specifically for reaching multicultural groups of women. With an increasing growth of outlets, such as YouTube, Facebook, Twitter, Instagram, and personal websites, one might believe many more practitioners, educators, scholars, and fitness enthusiasts would utilize such venues to spread evidence-based teachings of mental and physical health to prevent and reduce the growing obesity epidemic.

In recent years, I (Nina Ellis-Hervey- BeautifulBrwnBabyDol) have utilized discussions and digital story-telling on Facebook and YouTube of my own 100-pound weight loss, maintenance, and holistic health initiatives and intertwined the talks with psychological theories of self-esteem, self-efficacy, and locus of control and their role in the weight loss and weight maintenance process. These talks have been very popular with various populations but have been most effective in reaching multicultural women. Various blogs and

Facebook pages are dedicated to these efforts, such as "Black Women Workout", "Black Girls Run!", and various others. Collection of data from these populations (multicultural women) informs practice and assists in seeking the best methods for increasing interest in fitness and health for the "everyday" woman. This information is spread through platforms such as YouTube, Facebook, Twitter, Tumblr Blogs, and more.

Review of the Literature
Obesity in the United States of America has nearly tripled in the last 20 years, with over 34.9% of Americans identified as obese (Center for Disease Control [CDC], 2015). This is a dangerous and costly epidemic as obesity has been linked to conditions of heart disease, stroke, cancers, and diabetes (type 2). Annually, it is estimated to cost over 147 billion dollars in medical fees, which is 1,429 dollars higher than those of normal weight (CDC, 2015). Examination of obesity rates in the United States includes breaking down populations in terms of socioeconomic status and race/ethnicity. For race/ethnicity rates, non-Hispanic Blacks have the highest age-adjusted rate of obesity at 47.8%, with Hispanics closely behind at 42.5%, non-Hispanic Whites at 32.6%, and non-Hispanic Asians at 10.8% (CDC, 2015). In socioeconomic status rates, it poses an interesting breakdown. At the higher income levels, non-Hispanic Black and Mexican-American men have reportedly higher obesity rates than those with lower income (CDC, 2015). Yet with women, this report is opposite, and women who have a higher income are less likely to be listed as obese as those in a lower income status. Only among women is there a correlation between obesity and education level, where those with college degrees are less likely than those with lower education to be obese (CDC, 2015).

Different social media outlets. Social media sites have increased in popularity over the last 20 years, expanding and reaching multiple people in a variety of environments. Although trends with social media change on a regular basis, many websites have established a strong platform of cutting edge intrigue, enticing individuals to remain engaged on social media outlets. The U. S. Traffic Rank and

Global Traffic Rank website have tracked and maintained insight on the top 15 websites that are most used on the Internet (The eBusiness, 2016). These top 15 sites, in order, are Facebook, Twitter, LinkedIn, Pinterest, Google Plus+, Tumblr, Instagram, VK, Flickr, Vine, Meetup, Tagged, Ask.fm, MeetMe, and Classmates (eBusiness, 2016). Facebook ranks number one in a large margin, attracting over 1.1 billion visitors a month, followed by Twitter, attracting 3.1 million visitors monthly, and LinkedIn, which attracts 2.55 million monthly visitors.

Defining various terms.
Social media is defined as a form of electronic communication that maximizes social networking, blogging, microblogging, and vlogging to share information, personal beliefs and ideas, and other various content ("Social media", 2015). To better understand how social media works, identifying and analyzing the various forms of electronic communication is fundamental. Blogging is typically a website (such as Blogspot) in which individual's express personal opinions, activities, experiences, ideas, and thoughts in a typed format ("Blogging", 2015). Microblogging is similar to blogging but with a limit on characters and words, with frequent posting ("Microblogging", 2015). Vlogging takes another step in electronic communication of blogging by expressing these opinions, ideas, experiences, and activities through the form of a video ("Vlogging", 2015). The content and presentation may often differ with various forms of social networking but the main point is the same: to share ideas, discuss present and past activities, experiences, thoughts, feelings, and opinions about life experiences.

Identifying the populations using social media. Social media's expansion and permeation in most all aspects of life has begun to effect the way we interact with one another in terms of friends, families, and other relationships, including our doctors, mental health professionals, school teachers, children, and businesses. The provision of a way to connect via social networking allows quicker access to a range of opportunities that were not available 30 years ago. This access has changed much of the way the medical health profession utilizes social media, as many users become more advanced in understanding technology, their demands for at-your-fingertips-knowledge of health and information increases. Indeed, over 72% of adult Internet users are on Facebook, equaling over 62% of the adult population worldwide (Duggan, 2015). Instagram, Twitter, Pinterest, and LinkedIn have also attracted a significantly high number of the adult population, ranging from 23% of Internet users (Twitter) to 25% (LinkedIn), 28% (Instagram), and 31% (Pinterest) of adult Internet users. Further, in examining the most-used social media site of Facebook, 70% of these users are White (non-Hispanic), 67% Black (non-Hispanic), and 75% have identified as Hispanic and 66% are male while 77% have identified as female (Duggan, 2015). Health professionals in the mental health and medical fields have become increasingly aware of these statistics and its impact on the demand of communication between professionals and clients. Platforms such as "Hello Health" (created in Brooklyn), have developed a social media-type platform as a means of communicating to patients (Hawn, 2009). Hawn (2009) states that applications such as these provide the opportunity to link one's individual electronic health record with a social network to increase communication between the client and professional and ensure they receive their information. Programs like these are increasing in demand, as health care is one of America's largest leading industries yet has been the slowest to response to communication and information technology (Hawn, 2009).

Alleviating obesity in multicultural women through social media. Massanari (2012) addressed key components to the best practices in blogging from the perspective as a writer for the Center for Digital Ethics and Policy. Authors of any blog must examine seven key topics in writing and consider the consequences of the following: transparency, attribution, responsibility, face, text, truth, and citizenship. Transparency is addressed as how much the author of the social media site is willing to reveal about oneself and whether the information shared is on a private platform (i.e., a select few users may read it, if any) or a public platform (i.e., open to all individuals), whether a real persona should be used or hidden behind a moniker, can others comment (this may invite negative feedback), will those comments be moderated, will advertisements, sponsorship, or profit-sharing links be permitted, will a disclosure statement be included, and should a visitation track log be included to keep track of the type and location of people visiting the website. Attribution focuses on how a blogger may situate his or her work in relation to the sources they use and how they cite such sources. Responsibilities identifies how much responsibility a blogger takes in posting information and maintains a sense of social awareness, stays up-to-date on information, and remains accessible for viewers. This includes things such as frequency of blogging, accessibility of the blog, protecting the privacy rights of readers (i.e., collecting any personal information), what readers expect in response to comments, participation within the comments, and how a blogger handles any damaging statements made in a blog's comments. On the topic of face, Massanari (2012), addresses this as the voice the blogger wants to convey in discussing topics and the approach taken—Identifying on a professional or personal level with the audience. The author highlights that this is a spectrum and are not mutually exclusive. A blogger may still be professional with personal connections tied into it and vice versa. Another topic is examining the text, including images that will be used, video and audio, while still protecting creative content online. This includes acquiring permissions where necessary and avoiding copyright infringement, while still protecting the blogger's personal work as well. Truth and citizenship are the final two pieces to ethical practice in blogging. Truth highlights on honesty and conveying real situations and experiences to audience members and addressing new facts as data changes with a level of honesty that does not lead viewers to question the blogger's integrity. Citizenship focuses on the ability to serve as a public forum, holding a responsibility to be good public citizens and be cognizant of ethical responsibilities to the larger community-including a level of awareness of the audience and what is being said. A key point in citizenship is creating a formal (or possibly informal) policy of how to handle any disclosure of private information (Massanari, 2012). When targeting the main audience on social networking sites as a means to combat obesity within the larger community, it is advised to keep these seven key points in blogging in mind, applying it to vlogging, microblogging, and other communicative means of dispersing information. Addressing an audience and identifying ways to reduce obesity means being sensitive and aware of what the community needs, and not criticizing individuals who are considered obese or overweight. Often, individuals within the community seeking assistance in weight loss techniques have spent a greater portion of their lives being shunned or teased for their weight classifications. An awareness of this may discourage many bloggers from resorting to calling those individuals harsh names, or teasing them on any level but instead encourages them to provide positive supports that motivates them into losing weight and maintaining that weight loss. Identifying with readers through comments and responses of blog posts may contribute to this, as a blog who is abreast of their audience's needs, motivations, and desires may better target those in future communications.

> UNDERSTANDING THE MULTICULTURAL COMMUNITY HAS BECOME A NEW AND POSITIVE TREND IN THE 21ST CENTURY. THIS IS POSITIVE NEWS FOR AN UNDERSERVED COMMUNITY, AS MANY INDIVIDUALS, PARTICULARLY WOMEN, OF MULTICULTURAL BACKGROUND HAVE OFTEN BEEN PUSHED ASIDE OR FORCED TO RECONCILE WITH INCONSISTENCIES ON THEIR OWN.

Although recent research has reflected the inaccuracy of these reports, many statistical reports have displayed lower levels of depression and mental illness within ethnic communities other than White (Jack, Ali, & Dias, 2013). Nationally, reports have shown that Whites report higher levels of depression and anxiety compared to their counterparts of Black and Hispanic descent (CDC, 2013). Overall, though, it is statistically evident that women of multicultural background are at a much higher risk for mental illness because of their socioeconomic status, discrimination, lower education, larger families, poorer health, and an increased likelihood of single parenthood (APA, 2016). This risk does not change as women of multicultural background enter postsecondary education levels in the pursuit of higher education. Often, women of multicultural background are at higher risk when they enter the college settings, as they have minimal support, limited finances, and may come from an impoverished area (Lott, 2008). These risk factors put them at greater risk for developing mental illnesses of stress, depression, and anxiety.

Multicultural women in health and on the Internet. Large numbers of health-related blogs and vlogs are joining the ranks daily. More specifically, there are many, which target multicultural populations and more specifically women. Some of the larger known multicultural women blogs and vlogs include "A Black Girl's Guide to Weight Loss", "The Healthy Latina", "Black N' Fit", "Latino Fit Club", "Black Women Workout", "Black Girls Run!", "BeautifulBrwnBabyDol", and many more (Latina, 2016). These blogs and other mediums have risen with the aim of reducing the overwhelming increase in obesity-related illnesses, which has been observed in multicultural communities (Haupt, 2013).

> THE MANY WAYS IN WHICH FITNESS BLOGS AND VLOGS ARE BEING USED TO TACKLE OBESITY IN MULTICULTURAL COMMUNITIES VARY ACROSS SOCIAL MEDIUMS, WEBSITES, AND PRESENTATION.

Some blogs and vlogs urge readers and viewers to engage in healthy eating practices, team up with friends and partners, and even encourage them to attend "off screen" gathering and meetups, which aide in providing moral support, encouragement, and engagement in healthy living practices. One blog for example, "Black Girls Run!" (2016), states their blog and mission began to "Tackle the growing obesity epidemic in the African-American community and provide encouragement and resources to both new and veteran runners" (para. 3). They extend on this mission stating, "The mission of Black Girls RUN! is to encourage African-American women to make fitness and healthy living a priority" (para. 5). This blog, which was established in 2009, seeks to ensure that women have a network away from the blog. Followers are urged to join running teams in their own towns, create official meeting and running groups, socialize, and encourage one another to grow healthy and happy while improving the health statistics of women of color (Black Girls Run!, 2016).

Another example of such motivation is the blog "The Healthy Latina" (2016) which is an award-wining fitness blog started by Michelle Rivas, which is "… aimed at providing accurate and culturally-directed health information for Latinas" (para. 4). Rivas presents her readers with information about running and other vital workouts to motivate them to reach their own fitness goals. She also states that she "…is passionate about increasing the availability of culturally competent healthcare in the United States and hopes to conduct health communication research studies in underserved communities" (The Healthy Latina, 2016, para. 2). Such information and motivation assists in eliminating the obesity epidemic in targeted populations, while providing multicultural women with strength, confidence, and support from a person who is not only teaching a healthy approach, but living it.

A final example from the above listed, is the blog and vlog "BeautifulBrwnBabyDol". This blog and vlog, created by me, Dr. Nina Ellis-Hervey, utilizes my background as an Assistant Professor, psychologist, and researcher to create posts and videos that expound on my more than 100-pound weight loss (and maintenance), adoption, educational background, health, and natural hair care. I infuse my own life stories and psychology background to help others understand how I have completed each of these journeys, to provide readers and viewers with ways to gain self-esteem and self-confidence to complete journeys of their own. Further, I have collected an immense amount of research data from my viewing population when I have invited them to various speaking engagements, community events, and opportunities for them to ask me questions face-to-face in the presence of others who provide them support. Collection of such data has resulted in publications centered on discovering innovative methods to increase self-esteem and internal locus of control in multicultural women.

Conclusion
The use of social media to increase self-esteem and reduce the obesity epidemic has shown its relevance for various populations, more specifically, multicultural populations. In the review of

various established blogs and vlogs, and other social media sites, new motivational techniques are being developed daily. The overwhelming mentioned statistics on the populations utilizing social media has shown a significant influence in multicultural populations and beyond, further expounding the belief that the platforms of social media may be utilized as a key component in the battle against the growing epidemic of obesity, lack of self-esteem, internal locus of control, and mental illness overall.

Where do we go from here? In the future, a primary focus should be maintained on viewer interests by studying populations that are attracted to various websites, blogs, and vlogs, focused on health and fitness. Utilizing these mediums that have the highest amount of users and consistently promoting content dedicated to those social media users who need the help and information the most, will assist in reducing the obesity epidemic. A key component of every social media website focused on attracting and maintaining viewers is taking in viewer feedback, maintaining a level of transparency that allows users to connect, and providing a sense of security and safety that allows viewers to work on their self-esteem and locus of control. Although a majority of authors of blogs, vlogs, and other social media websites follow this demand of their viewers, it is important for future authors to disseminate public health information and continue to spread awareness of recent evidence-based articles on ways to combat obesity among multicultural women. A recommendation includes authors of popular websites partnering with doctors, mental health professionals, and other fitness experts to increase the transparency of effective healthy interventions that assist in the fight on obesity.

REFERENCES

American Heart Association. (2012). Social media may help fight childhood obesity. Retrieved from http://newsroom.heart.org/news/social-media-may-help-fight-childhood-241222

American Psychological Association. (2016). Women and depression. Retrieved from http://www.apa.org/about/gr/issues/women/depression.aspx
BeautifulBrwnBabyDol. (2016). How I lost 100 pounds: My hard transition from fat to skinny. Retrieved from https://www.youtube.com/user/BeautifulBrwnBabyDol

Black Girls Run! (2016). Welcome to the movement. Retrieved from http://blackgirlsrun.com/

Blogging (2015). In Merriam-Webster Online. Retrieved from http://www.merriam-webster.com/dictionary/blogging

Center for Disease Control (2015). Obesity is common, serious and costly. Retrieved from http://www.cdc.gov/obesity/data/adult.html

Duggan, M. (2015). The demographics of social media users. PewInternet. Retrieved from http://www.pewinternet.org/2015/08/19/the-demographics-of-social-media-users/

Hall, R. R., Francis, S. F., Whitt-Glover, M., Loftin-Bell, K., Swett, K., & McMichael, A. J. (2013). Hair care practices as a barrier to physical activity in African American women. JAMA Dermatol, 149(3), 310-314. doi: 10.1001/jamadermatol.2013.1946

Haupt, A. (2013). "Michelle Obama Speaks Out Against Childhood Obesity" U.S. News. http://health.usnews.com/health-news/health-wellness/articles/2013/03/11/michelle- obama-speaks out-against-childhood-obesity
Hawn, C. (2009) Take Two Aspirin and Tweet Me in the Morning. Health Affairs. 28 (2)   DOI 10.1377//hlthaff.28.2.361

Latina. (2016). The top 10 Latina health and fitness bloggers! Retrieved from http://www.latina.com/lifestyle/health/latina-health-fitness-bloggers

Massanari, A. L. (2012). Best practices for bloggers: Dimensions for consideration. Loyola University Chicago. Retrieved from http://digitalethics.org/resources/best-practices-for-bloggers-dimensions-for-consideration/

McLeod, S. (2007). Professors who blog: web 2.0 publishing venues don't need to clash with higher education's traditional practices. Technology & Learning, 27(10), 50.

Microblogging (2015). In Merriam-Webster Online. Retrieved from http://www.merriam-webster.com/dictionary/Microblogging

Social media (2015). In Merriam-Webster Online. Retrieved from http://www.merriam-webster.com/dictionary/social%20media

The eBusiness (2016). Top 15 most popular social networking sites. The eBusiness. Retrieved from http://www.ebizmba.com/articles/social-networking-websites
The Healthy Latina. (2016). About. Retrieved from http://www.thehealthylatina.com/about/

Vlogging (2015). In Merriam-Webster Online. Retrieved from http://www.merriam- webster.com/dictionary/vlogging

Walker, J. (2006). "Blogging From Inside the Ivory Tower". In Bruns, A. & Jacobs, J. (Eds.), Uses of blogs, 127-138. Digital Formations 38. New York: Peter Lang Publishing.

Biography of Nina Ellis

Dr. Nina Ellis-Hervey a.k.a. BeautifulBrwnBabyDol is a tenured and Associate Professor in the School Psychology Doctoral Program at Stephen F. Austin State University. She is a Licensed Psychologist, Nationally Certified School Psychologist, a Licensed Specialist in School Psychology in the state of Texas and a Certified Professional Life Coach. She is also the director of the School Psychology Assessment Center on campus. She is soon to be a Certified Personal Trainer in 2017. Her YouTube channels and website entitled "BeautifulBrwnBabyDol" and "BeautifulBrwnBabyDolTV" chronicle her more than 100lb. weight loss she has maintained for over 10 years, educational triumphs, healthy psychological tips and beauty tutorials. With over half a million subscribers (between channels), millions of video views nationally and internationally, and nearly 1 million following across networks, Dr. Nina is making her mark on the world. Her YouTube channel has recently been named as a top 10 natural hair vlog by Buzzfeed. She has also been featured in PEOPLE, Essence and Ebony magazines and the TV shows HLN News Live, the Jeff Probst Show, Inside Edition, Extra, The Grio, Refinery 29 and more! She was named a St. Louis Woman Power Player by Delux Magazine as well! Dr. Nina has even given a TED talk at the Illinois Institute of Technology. She has also spoken at many universities including Howard University, Colgate University, Albany State University, Texas State University, Illinois State University and more. Her academic works have been and are being published in the journals Learning, Media and Technology, Journal of Human Services, Educational Review, The McNair Scholarly Review, Psychology Discourse, Journal of Black Studies, Journal of Multicultural Affairs and Girls Like Us: Risk, Resilience and Healthy Development of Diverse Girls. She believes in supporting others in reaching their goals and seeing their lives as valuable in spite of any adversity they may face. She lives her life as the ultimate example of that.

The goal of this book has been to address how women's issues of self-perception and body image affect their identity and confidence.

Each woman must find her beauty.

And ultimately women must learn not to change so that people will like them.

Rather the goal is to be yourself and the right people will love you.

About the Contributors

Nina Ellis, PhD is a young Doctorate-Level School Psychologist, Professor at Stephen F. Austin State University, Vlogger, Blogger and Motivational Speaker aspiring to rid the world of their lack of motivation by educating them about hair, skin care, weight loss and true acceptance of self.

Candace Liger is the CEO of #GoodFunk HeadQuarters, an organization that emphasizes fun and unique opportunities to achieve optimal health, wellness, and creative expression. Her current positions include: NASM Certified Fitness Eccentric, group fitness instructor, nationally recognized spoke word poet, performance artist, exclusive fitness blogger for the Poets Without Limits Online Magazine, social activist, dancer, and mother of two glorious children.

Allyson Reneau is a business woman, gymnastics coach and judge, and is mother to 11 children. After putting off a lifelong dream of finishing her education, she enrolled at the University of Oklahoma and completed 76 hours in just 3 semesters to finish her BA in Communications with a 4.0 GPA......all while juggling 7 kids at home and running a highly competitive gymnastics program training Olympic hopefuls. Allyson has worked with hundreds of state, regional, and national gymnastics champions.

In Fall 2011, at the age of 50, she entered the Masters program at Harvard in the field of International Relations. She travels 4000 miles weekly between her base in Oklahoma City and Boston for her classes. She currently maintains a 4.0 and plans to finish her degree in the Fall of 2015. In addition, Allyson auditioned at Juilliard (piano) in January of 2012 and has been attending for 3 semesters. Allyson has been invited to the United Nations several times to meet with the Executive Director of Worldwide Humanitarian Projects and the Director of Protection for Women and Children. She has a dream to help as many women and girls as possible to find their purpose in life through education and entrepreneurship.

Also, she has just completed a joint research project between Harvard and the Naval War College on "Mentoring in the Military." This article was recently published in two journals. To give substance to her emerging interest in space activities, Allyson was a participant in the 2014 Space Studies Program of the International Space University in Montreal, Canada, and returned as a Teaching Assistant for the 2015 program held at Ohio University in Athens, Ohio. Allyson has been featured on FOX News, NBC, ABC, the Today Show, and in countless magazines and newspapers around the world.

Julie Shapiro has been in the fitness industry for 10 years in a variety of roles. She has been a weight loss consultant for a major weight loss company, certified personal trainer, yoga teacher and group exercise instructor. Julie has a Bachelors Degree of Arts in Psychology and a Bachelors Degree of Science in Hospitality, Food Management and Science Studies. She has worked with a variety of women to help them achieve their goals in a healthy and non-aggressive manner. Helping women and girls see fitness as a means to be healthy and set goals that are attainable are some of the things that

beYOUtiful

www.beyoutifulbooks.com

Julie works on with her clients. Her goal is to help her clients reach their goals!

Jennifer Armstrong is a Certified Nutrition and Wellness Consultant and Nutritionist, with an Associates of Arts Degree in Enterprise Development. She works part-time as a fitness instructor at the Midwest City YMCA and enjoys volunteering as a Youth Soccer Coach. She is working on obtaining a B.S. in Nutrition and Dietetics from the University of Central Oklahoma. She is the "Eat Clean" half of No Excuses OKC, along with personal trainer and exercise specialist Stenia Little. Her passion is to help other women and children live healthy, happy lives through nutrition education, fitness, and total mind, body, and spirit wellness.

Carlie Carpio is a USC Marshall School of Business Graduate, yogi, certified personal trainer, foodie, traveler, an avid reader, and a lover of life. She founded RegularGirlFitness when she realized that she was unhappy and had not been making her health a priority. RGF serves as a chronicle of her journey and to inspire others, as well as herself, that you can get healthy, stay fit, and still have a life too. Fitness isn't just about the abs; it's about being fit in every facet of your life...

Dee Dee Grayson is the very blessed mom of Jesse, Jerece, JaLeisa, Jade, Jerry II, Joshua and Josiah. Grandmother of Luke and the precious wife of Jerry Sr. She loves singing, reading, drawing, photography, scrapbooking and traveling! Dee Dee began her birth work journey in 2014 by becoming a Certified Lactation Counselor. She has served as the COBA Baby Cafe Assistant Director and Facilitator in the minority program. Dee Dee serves families through her business Bountiful Blessings Birth and Postpartum Doula Services. She supports and nurtures as the families prepare to meet their bundle(s) of joy. Dee Dee's plans for the future include travel and obtaining her IBCLC credential.

About the Editor

YAISA MANN

Body Image Expert, Professional Hype Girl and CEO of SwagHER Fitness, LLC and Pigeon Toed Publishing, LLC Yaisa Mann is leading the way blending body image, fun, positivity, and motivation to empower girls and women.

She has years of academic teaching and research experience holding a dual B.A. in English and African American Studies from California State University, Fresno; M.A. in English from her alma mater, and on her journey to completing a PhD in Interdisciplinary Studies from the University of Oklahoma. She holds countless fitness certifications: YMCA Group Fitness Certification, Healthy Lifestyle Wellness Coach Certification, YASA (YMCA Aquatic Safety Assistant) Certification and is licensed to teach Zumba Basic 1, Zumba Basic 2, Zumba Toning, Aqua Zumba, Zumba Kids, Zumba Gold, Zumba Sentao, R.I.P.P.E.D., Turbo Kick, Hip Hop Hustle, and Bokwa just to name some of the hottest workout trends.

Yaisa not only follows the trends but also makes up her own! She created and taught the first course in body image ever taught at the University of Oklahoma in 2008 starting with the course Body Image versus Reality: Popular Culture and the Beauty Myth; she was selected to be featured in the 40th Anniversary Edition of Our Bodies, Ourselves (2011); was selected to be featured in the National Eating Disorders Association Awareness Month Calendar Campaign (2013) for her body image advocacy; was selected to be a speaker for the Great Night of the Orators at the University of Oklahoma (2013); won the

University of Oklahoma Inaugural Brightest Idea Speaker Symposium Contest (2013), invited to serve as a board member for the Oklahoma Eating Disorders Association (2014), and was recently invited to the Dillard's pace setters winner's circle as a beauty advisor for Kiehl's (2016).

Her interest in body image and fitness came directly out of her own personal experiences with her brown skin color, curly and frizzy hair texture with lots of shrinkage, junk food binge eating, battle with maintaining a healthy weight and overall struggle with self-acceptance and being who God made her to be. Although she has struggled to see her own beauty feeling the pressure from cultural influences like the color complex and media pressures, she has always felt empowered and free to live by her own rules through dance.

Her passion for dance inspired her to start her own women's wellness SwagHER Fitness. In order to promote a healthy self esteem and body image in girls and women SwagHER Fitness incorporates popular and effective workouts like Zumba, boot camp, aqua fitness, hip hop, and (online and face-to-face) personal and group coaching. Yaisa can be booked for your next big event that needs an energizer through fitness, motivational speaking or a healthy dose of a body image seminar! She invites you to start loving your body by living by your own rules!

A California native, Yaisa currently resides in the Norman, OK with her family. Her children Jalen, Josiah, and Jael are her inspiration and her joy.

Contact information: Yaisa Mann
Phone: 405.473.1566
Email: yaisa@swagherfitness.com
Website: www.swagherfitness.com

Discussion Questions

1. Describe how do you see yourself in 3 words.
   _____
   _____

2. Describe how your family would describe you in 3 words.
   _____

3. Describe how your friends would describe you in 3 words.
   _____

4. Write down what you would like to see or who you would like to be.
   _____

5. What is stopping you from seeing or being this?
   _____

6. What are your closest/strained relationships like?
   _____
   _____

"When I look at you, I see myself.
If my eyes are unable to see you as my sister,
it is because my own vision is blurred.
And if that be so, then it is I who need you either because
I do not understand who you are, my sister, or because
I need you to help me understand who I am."

LILLIAN PIERCE BENBOW
PAST NATIONAL PRESIDENT OF DELTA SIGMA THETA SORORITY, INC.
1971-1975

Made in the USA
Columbia, SC
28 September 2020